GETTING TO KNOW ENGINEERING GENRES

エンジニアのための総合英語

AKIKO MIYAMA
ATSUSHI MUKUHIRA
TOMOKO TSUJIMOTO
ASHLEY MOORE
ERIK FRITZ
TANYA MCCARTHY

SANSHUSHA

写真提供

p. 11　　　　　The Washington Post
p. 22（左）　　トヨタ車体株式会社
p. 22（中央）　日産自動車株式会社
p. 22（右）　　本田技研工業株式会社
p. 30　　　　　©iStockphoto.com/nazarethman
p. 46　　　　　©iStockphoto.com/CinematicFilm
p. 63　　　　　The Washington Post

はじめに

　急速に進むグローバル化によって、世界に情報を発信していく力が今まで以上に求められるようになってきました。さまざまな新しい技術が開発され世に出ていますが、良い技術を持っていても、発信する力がなければ、世間に認められるチャンスが少なくなります。科学技術とは、あらゆる物理的問題に対するひとつの解決策、もしくは解決策を生み出すための人間的努力の結晶、そして人類が積み重ねてきた技術の歴史の集積でもあります。

　本書は、主に理工系の学生の皆さんが、科学技術の様々な分野の情報を英語で理解するのに必要な基礎力を養う目的で作られています。各先端技術分野においてどのような研究がなされ、どのような製品が開発されているのかを学べるなど、英語で情報を理解し、発信する際に必要となるコミュニケーションの各ジャンルの特徴を学習できます。本書を学習することでグローバルに活躍することができる技術者として、様々なシチュエーションに対応できる英語力を身につけることができるでしょう。

本書の構成と使い方

　各 Chapter は以下の項目で構成されています。

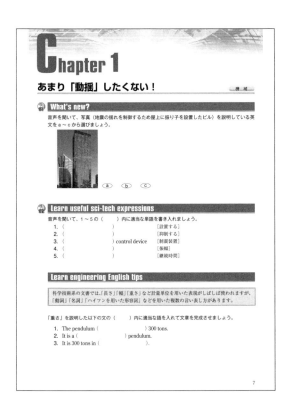

What's new?

ウォームアップのためのリスニング問題です。各章のトピックに関連した写真やイラストを見て、写真を正しく表している英文を選びます。**どのようなトピックなのか概観できる問題**となっています。

Learn useful sci-tech expressions

後続セクションのウォームアップ問題です。本文に出てくる**理工系専門用語**が取り上げられており、意味と発音を確認します。

Learn engineering English tips

理工系の英文に**頻出する語法や文法**についての問題です。

Get information

英字新聞に掲載された、さまざまな**専門分野の最先端技術を紹介した記事**を素材としたリーディングのセクションです。難解な表現には注がついていますが、意味が分からない場合に参照する程度にし、できるだけ意味を類推しながら読むよう心がけてください。

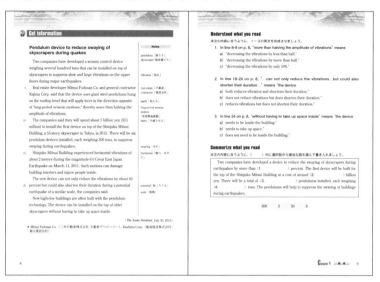

Understand what you read

リーディングセクションの**内容理解を確認する問題**です。True or False や多肢選択肢問題で、内容が理解できているかどうかをチェックしてください。

Summarize what you read

リーディングセクションの内容理解を**要約**で確認するセクションです。要約することにより、内容をより深く確実に理解し、言い換え表現も学べます。

Get to know engineering genres

英語で発信する力を養うセクションです。このセクションは、さまざまなジャンルの英文素材を取り上げ、その**ジャンルに特有の表現形式や語法**について学びます。リーディングセクションのトピックに関連する資料の実例を用いた読解問題やリスニング問題となっています。

Table of Contents

専門分野

Chapter 1 あまり「動揺」したくない！　　　　　　　　　　　　　機械
Pendulum device to reduce swaying of skyscrapers during quakes　　7

Chapter 2 マインドコントロールにご用心！　　　　　　　　　　　脳科学
Experiment lets man use his mind to control another person's movements　　11

Chapter 3 3Dプリンターで臓器を作製　　　　　　　　　　　　　医療工学
Researchers create 'bionic ear'　　15

Chapter 4 超小型EV車がデビュー　　　　　　　　　　　　　　　機械
Ultra minicars take to public roads　　19

Chapter 5 進化するポータブル・デバイス　　　　　　　　　　機械・電気
Japan, overseas firms battle over wearable tech business　　23

Chapter 6 癌を検知する「賢いメス」　　　　　　　　　　　　　医療工学
New surgical knife can detect cancer instantly　　27

Chapter 7 緊急時に「光る」モノ　　　　　　　　　　　　　　　化　学
Hakko Giken, university jointly develop luminescent gel　　31

Chapter 8 超電導リニア登場　　　　　　　　　　　　　　　　電気・機械
Deep secrets of maglev Shinkansen emerging　　35

Chapter 9 手のひらであなたが分かる　　　　　　　　　　　　情報・機械
A new palm vein ID system creates codes for multiple services　　39

Chapter 10 国際基準を作って産業育成　　　　　　　　　　　　医療工学
ISO to adopt Japan-led safety criteria for nursing-care robots　　43

Chapter 11 もはや「運転手」はいらない？　　　　　　　　　　　電　子
Nissan rolls out self-driving car at Japanese electronics show　　47

Chapter 12　親離れする日は近い?!　　機　械
Robots are getting closer to having humanlike abilities and senses　　51

Chapter 13　気体の錬金術で夢の新材料を　　化　学
Nanotech scientist aspires to master 'alchemy of gases'　　55

Chapter 14　再生可能エネルギー導入拡大への鍵　　電気・エネルギー
Big battery eyed as green energy cure　　59

Chapter 15　新しい生命体を作り出す企業　　バイオ
Scientists now creating millions of organisms from scratch　　63

Chapter 16　スパコンで天気予報　　電　子
Japanese supercomputer shows detailed cloud movements on Earth's surface　　67

Chapter 17　スマホと嗅覚の香しい関係　　機　械
Firm wants your smartphone to be able to smell　　71

Chapter 18　高齢化社会に強力な助っ人　　機　械
Robot wheelchairs would read users' minds　　75

Chapter 19　食品偽装を見破るソフト　　情　報
Kyoto researchers develop DNA software that can halt food fraud　　79

Chapter 20　もしかして万能波長？　　機械・物理
Industries studying possible next big thing: Terahertz waves　　83

Chapter 21　洋上風力発電は未来を照らす？　　エネルギー
Japan starts up offshore wind farm near Fukushima　　87

Chapter 22　コンピュータが常識を持つ？　　情　報
New research aims to teach computers common sense　　91

Chapter 1

あまり「動揺」したくない！

機 械

What's new?

音声を聞いて、写真（地震の揺れを制御するため屋上に振り子を設置したビル）を説明している英文をa～cから選びましょう。

ⓐ   ⓑ   ⓒ

Learn useful sci-tech expressions

音声を聞いて、1～5の（　　　）内に適当な単語を書き入れましょう。

1. (　　　　　　　　　)　　　　　　　［設置する］
2. (　　　　　　　　　)　　　　　　　［抑制する］
3. (　　　　　　　　) control device　［制震装置］
4. (　　　　　　　　　)　　　　　　　［振幅］
5. (　　　　　　　　　)　　　　　　　［継続時間］

Learn engineering English tips

科学技術系の文書では、「長さ」「幅」「重さ」など計量単位を用いた表現がしばしば使われますが、「動詞」「名詞」「ハイフンを用いた形容詞」などを用いた複数の言い表し方があります。

「重さ」を説明した以下の文の（　　　）内に適当な語を入れて文章を完成させましょう。

1. The pendulum (　　　　　　　　　) 300 tons.
2. It is a (　　　　　　　) pendulum.
3. It is 300 tons in (　　　　　　　).

Get information

Pendulum device to reduce swaying of skyscrapers during quakes

Two companies have developed a seismic control device weighing several hundred tons that can be installed on top of skyscrapers to suppress slow and large vibrations on the upper floors during major earthquakes.

Real estate developer Mitsui Fudosan Co. and general contractor Kajima Corp. said that the device uses giant steel pendulums hung on the rooftop level that will apply force in the direction opposite of "long-period seismic motions," thereby more than halving the amplitude of vibrations.

The companies said they will spend about 5 billion yen ($51 million) to install the first device on top of the Shinjuku Mitsui Building, a 55-story skyscraper in Tokyo, in 2015. There will be six pendulum devices installed, each weighing 300 tons, to suppress swaying during earthquakes.

Shinjuku Mitsui Building experienced horizontal vibrations of about 2 meters during the magnitude-9.0 Great East Japan Earthquake on March 11, 2011. Such motions can damage building interiors and injure people inside.

The new device can not only reduce the vibrations by about 60 percent but could also shorten their duration during a potential earthquake of a similar scale, the companies said.

New high-rise buildings are often built with the pendulum technology. The device can be installed on the top of older skyscrapers without having to take up space inside.

(*The Asahi Shimbun*, July 30, 2013)

Notes

pendulum「振り子」
skyscraper「超高層ビル」

vibration「揺れ」

real estate「不動産」
contractor「建設会社」

apply「加える」

long-period seismic motion「長周期地震動」
halve「半減させる」

swaying「ゆれ」
horizontal「横の、水平の」

potential「起こりうる」
scale「規模」

* Mitsui Fudosan Co.（三井不動産株式会社：不動産デベロッパー）、Kajima Corp.（鹿島建設株式会社：総合建設会社）

Understand what you read

本文の内容に合うように、1～3の英文を完成させましょう。

1. In lines 8-9 on p. 8, "more than halving the amplitude of vibrations" means
    a) decreasing the amplitude of vibrations by less than half.
    b) decreasing the amplitude of vibrations by more than half.
    c) decreasing the amplitude of vibrations by only 50%.

2. In lines 19-20 on p. 8, "...can not only reduce the vibrations…but could also shorten their duration…" means the device
    a) both reduces vibration and shortens their duration.
    b) does not reduce vibrations but does shorten their duration.
    c) reduces vibrations but does not shorten their duration.

3. In line 24 on p. 8, "without having to take up space inside" means the device
    a) needs to be inside the building.
    b) needs to take up space.
    c) does not need to be inside the building.

Summarize what you read

本文の内容に合うように、(　　　)内に選択肢から適当な語を選んで書き入れましょう。

Two companies have developed a device to reduce the swaying of skyscrapers during earthquakes by more than (1.　　　　) percent. The first device will be built for the top of the Shinjuku Mitsui Building at a cost of around (2.　　　　) billion yen. There will be a total of (3.　　　　) pendulums installed, each weighing (4.　　　　) tons. The pendulums will help to suppress the swaying of buildings during earthquakes.

　　　　300　　　5　　　50　　　6

Get to know engineering genres

Target Genre ▶ **Figure**

図版には図を説明するキャプションがつけられます。キャプション中の英語は、**文よりも句や複合名詞（ハイフンでつながれた形容詞相当語句を伴う）**が好まれます。

次の図版を参照しながら、以下の英文の（　　）内に選択肢より適当な語句を選び書き入れましょう。

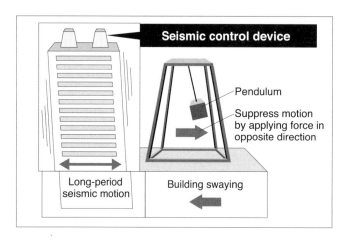

　The (1.　　　　　　), which has a pendulum, can be installed on the roof of very tall buildings. When a (2.　　　　　　) happens, a building can start to move, or sway, from one side to another. This movement is called "(3.　　　　　　) seismic motion." The pendulum on top of the building, however, will start to move in the opposite direction of the (4.　　　　　　). For example, if the building sways to the left, the pendulum will sway to the right. The weight of the pendulum and the force it provides act to reduce the amount of sway and vibration the building experiences. Thus, the long-period seismic motion is (5.　　　　　　) by this device.

　　long-period　　greatly reduced　　seismic control device

　　　　swaying building　　large earthquake

Chapter 2
マインドコントロールにご用心！

脳科学

What's new?

音声を聞いて、写真を説明している英文をa～cから選びましょう。

ⓐ　ⓑ　ⓒ

Learn useful sci-tech expressions

音声を聞いて、1～5の（　）内に適当な単語を書き入れましょう。

1. （　　　　　　　　）　　　　　　［電極］
2. （　　　　　　　　）　　　　　　［連結装置］
3. （　　　　　　　　）brain signal　［電気的な脳信号］
4. （　　　　　　　　）　　　　　　［脳科学者］
5. （　　　　　　　　）　　　　　　［埋め込む］

Learn engineering English tips

> 実験などを説明する際に以下の表現がしばしば使われます。
> one ... another ... 「ひとつは～で、もうひとつは～」（総数不定）
> one ... the other ... 「ひとつは～で、他方は～」（総数限定）

以下の文章の（　）内に適当な語句を書き入れましょう。

　Two people participated in the experiment. (**1.**　　　　　　　) man looked at a computer game on a screen and thought about what move he wanted to make. Almost instantaneously, (**2.**　　　　　　) who couldn't see the screen, moved his right index finger to make that move.

Notes: instantaneously「すぐに」　move「動き」　index finger「人指し指」

Get information

Experiment lets man use his mind to control another person's movements

    So it turns out a bit of mind control might be possible after all. Scientists had already shown that a human could send an electronic brain signal to a rat, prompting it to wiggle its tail. Now, two University of Washington researchers say they have
5 demonstrated that one person's thoughts can control another person's movements.

    First, electrodes were placed against the subject's head. The first subject then looked at a computer game on a screen and thought about what move he wanted to make. The second subject,
10 sitting on the other side of the campus but connected to the first subject via the Internet and a brain stimulation device, almost instantaneously moved his right index finger to make that move. He said it had the sensation of a nervous tic.

    In the past two decades, neuroscientists have made dramatic
15 advances in connecting human brains with computers, largely in the hope of helping disabled and paralyzed patients communicate with others and operate prosthetic limbs.

    The previous brain-to-brain interfaces involved electrodes implanted directly into rat brains. "This is the first noninvasive
20 brain-to-brain interface," said Rajesh Rao, the computational neuroscientist whose brain sent the signal.

    Neurobiologist Miguel Nicolelis at Duke University, who in February reported that he and his colleagues linked two rat brains together across continents, said this latest research is
25 rudimentary at best. "This is more like one brain sending an electric shock to another than a true interface," Nicolelis said.

(by Charles Q. Choi, *The Washington Post*, Aug. 29, 2013)

Notes

turn out「〜だと分かる」

prompt...to〜「…に〜するよう促す」
wiggle「振る」
demonstrate「実証する」

subject「被験者」

sensation「感覚」
nervous tic「神経の痙攣」
neuroscientist「神経科学者」
largely「主に」
disabled「身体に障害を抱えた」
paralyzed「麻痺した」
prosthetic limbs「人工の四肢」
previous「以前の」
noninvasive「非侵襲性の」
neurobiologist「神経生物学者」
colleague「同僚」
rudimentary「芽が出た段階」
at best「せいぜい」

Understand what you read

本文を読み、質問に答えましょう。

1. Who does this research mainly aim to help?
   a) disabled people
   b) neuroscientists
   c) researchers
   d) gamers

2. Over how many years have advances in human brain-to-computer interfaces been made?
   a) two years
   b) ten years
   c) twenty years
   d) twelve years

3. In this articles, what does the author mean by mind control?
   a) The ability of a computer to control the movements of a human
   b) The ability of an animal to control the movements of a human
   c) The ability of a human to control the movements of a human
   d) The ability of a human to control the movements of a computer

Summarize what you read

本文の内容に合うように、（　　）内に選択肢から適当な語を選んで書き入れましょう。

> Over the past two decades, neuroscience has shown (1.　　　　　) in the area of mind control. University of Washington researchers used electrodes to link the (2.　　　　　) of two human research subjects and showed that one subject's thoughts could control the other's (3.　　　　　). In previous studies, (4.　　　　　) were implanted directly into rat brains. However, recent research allows the electrodes to be fitted noninvasively.

movements　　electrodes　　advances　　brains

Get to know engineering genres

Target Genre ▶ **Flow Chart**

Flow Chart（フローチャート）は、プロセスを説明するときにしばしば用いられます。フローチャートは一目でプロセスを理解させるための工夫のひとつです。図の解説には、しばしば**名詞句**が用いられるのが特徴です。

音声を聞いて、Flow Chart で説明されているプロセス中の (a) ～ (e) は、以下のどの項目に該当するか、〔　　　〕内に書き入れましょう。

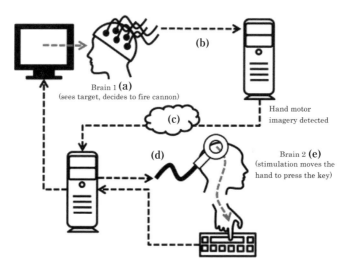

Figure: Brain-to-brain communication between two subjects via a computer game

(a) 〔　　　　　　　　　　　　　　　〕
(b) 〔　　　　　　　　　　　　　　　〕
(c) 〔　　　　　　　　　　　　　　　〕
(d) 〔　　　　　　　　　　　　　　　〕
(e) 〔　　　　　　　　　　　　　　　〕

EEG Recording of Brain Activity

Sender　　　Internet　　　Receiver

Brain Stimulation using TMS

Notes: EEG（electroencephalogram）「脳波図、脳電図」　TMS（transcranial magnetic stimulation）「経頭蓋磁気刺激法」

Chapter 3

3Dプリンターで臓器を作製

医療工学

What's new?

音声を聞いて、写真（3Dプリンターで作製した、軟骨を伴ったコイル状のアンテナが付いている人工耳で、シャーレに入っている）を説明している英文をa～cから選びましょう。

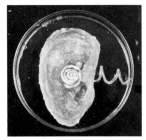

ⓐ　ⓑ　ⓒ

Photo：Mel Evans, AP

Learn useful sci-tech expressions

音声を聞いて、1～5の（　　）内に適当な単語を書き入れましょう。

1. Petri (　　　　　　)　　［シャーレ］
2. liquid (　　　　　　)　　［液体ゲル］
3. (　　　　　　)　　［電子工学］
4. (　　　　　　)　　［微小な粒］
5. (　　　　　　)　　［培養する］

Learn engineering English tips

実験手続きなどの指示文には命令文が使用されます。また、禁止事項を指示する場合は、「Do not ＋命令文」の構文を使用します。

以下の1～3の指示文の（　　）内に、選択肢から適当な語句を選んで書き入れましょう。なお、文頭にくる語も小文字で示しています。

1. (　　　　　　) the Petri dish with liquid.
2. (　　　　　　) electrodes onto the backs of the ears.
3. Do not (　　　　　　) the power supply.

attach　　shut off　　fill

Get information

Researchers create 'bionic ear'

With a 3D printer, a Petri dish and some cells from a cow, Princeton University researchers are growing synthetic ears that can receive sound.

The scientists send bovine cells mixed in a liquid gel through the printer, followed by tiny particles of silver. The printer is programmed to shape the material into a "bionic ear," and forms the silver particles into a coiled antenna. Like any antenna, this one can pick up radio signals that the ear will interpret as sound.

The 3D ear is not designed to replace a human one, though; the research is meant to explore a new method of combining electronics with biological material.

"What we really did here was actually prove the capabilities of 3D printing," said Michael McAlpine, the professor who led the project. "Because most people use 3D printing to print such things as figurines and jewelry."

After it is printed, the 3D ear is soft and translucent. It is cultivated for 10 weeks, letting the cells multiply, creating a flesh color and forming hardened tissue around the antenna.

Manu Mannoor, a graduate student who worked with McAlpine on the project, held up a Petri dish in a lab at Princeton last week to show how the process works. The dish was filled with liquid and a partly cultivated ear.

McAlpine said, "As the world becomes a more digital and electronic place, I think ultimately we're going to care less about our traditional five senses," he said. "And we're going to want these new senses to give us direct electronic communication with our cellphones and our laptop devices."

(By Keith Collins and Kathy Matheson, Associated Press, July 3, 2013)

＊Princeton University（プリンストン大学：アメリカのニュージャージー州にある大学）

Notes

synthetic「合成の」

bovine「牛の」

coiled「コイル状の」
interpret「解釈する」
replace「置き換える」
explore「探る」

prove「証明する」

figurine「小さな像」
jewelry「宝飾品」
translucent「半透明の」
multiply「増殖する」
flesh color「肌色」
tissue「組織」

ultimately「最終的に」

Understand what you read

本文の内容に合うものには T (True) を、合わないものには F (False) を (　　) 内に書き入れましょう。

1. (　　) The synthetic ear was made using cells taken from an animal.

2. (　　) The researchers are going to try and implant the ears onto humans.

3. (　　) The research will allow manufacturers to create bionic jewelry.

4. (　　) The ear changes color over time during the cultivation process.

5. (　　) Manu Mannoor was the researcher in charge of the project.

Summarize what you read

本文の内容に合うように、(　　) 内に選択肢から適当な語を選んで書き入れましょう。

Researchers have succeeded in using a 3D printer to combine biological and electronic material to create a (1.　　　　　) "ear." Moving away from (2.　　　　　) uses of 3D printers, the team managed to print an ear that could pick up radio signals through a (3.　　　　　) metal antenna. The (4.　　　　　) researcher suggested that one day this type of technology could be used to allow humans to communicate directly with electronic machines.

traditional　　synthetic　　connected　　lead

Get to know engineering genres

Target Genre ▶ **Presentation slide**

パワーポイントなどのプレゼンテーション用ソフトウェアを使ってプレゼンテーションを行う場合、スライド中の表現は、聴衆が瞬時に判断しやすいように**簡単な構文を使い**、メッセージを入れすぎないようにします。

以下のスライドを参照しながらプレゼンテーション（ベートーベンの『エリーゼのために』を人工耳に聞かせる実験プロセスの説明）を聞き、スライド中のa～cに当てはまる語句を選択肢から選んで書き入れましょう。

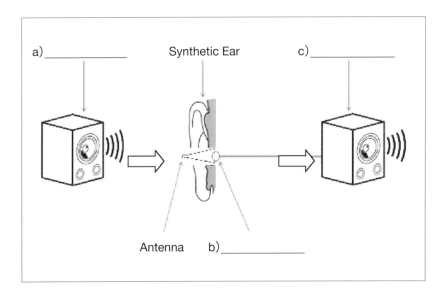

speaker   sound source   electrode

Chapter 4

超小型 EV 車がデビュー

機 械

What's new?

音声を聴いて、図の製品について説明している英文を a ～ c から選びましょう。

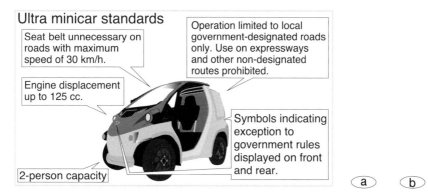

ⓐ   ⓑ   ⓒ

Learn useful sci-tech expressions

音声を聞いて、1 ～ 5 の（　　）内に適当な単語を書き入れましょう。

1. (　　　　　　　　) vehicle　　　［従来型の車］
2. (　　　　　　　　) speed　　　　［最高速度］
3. main (　　　　　　　　)　　　　　［主要特長］
4. (　　　　　　　　) model　　　　［試作モデル］
5. (　　　　　　　　) efficiency　　［燃費］

Learn engineering English tips

技術文書では、数量の基準に用いられる単位は記号で示されることが多いです。頻出の単位記号は意味を覚えておきましょう。

1 ～ 4 の単位記号について、例を参考にして（　　）内に語句を書き入れましょう。

例　cm　(centimeter(s))　［センチメートル］

1. cc　　(　　　　　　　　)　[　　　　　　　]
2. km/h　(　　　　　　　　)　[　　　　　　　]
3. mpm　(　　　　　　　　)　[　　　　　　　]
4. sqm　(　　　　　　　　)　[　　　　　　　]

Get information

Ultra minicars take to public roads

Ultra minicars, which are one- or two-seater vehicles smaller than conventional minicars, have begun running on public roads in Japan. Using prototype models, automakers certified by the Land, Infrastructure, Transport and Tourism Ministry are conducting road tests over a trial period of about two years.

Consumer models of ultra minicars will likely debut in fiscal 2015 at the earliest. The government plans to promote the widespread use of ultra minicars, which boast high fuel efficiency, in an effort to reduce carbon dioxide (CO_2) emissions.

The New Mobility Concept (NMC), Nissan Motor Co.'s ultra minicar prototype model, is an electric vehicle equipped with two seats. When two adult passengers are seated in the vehicle, there is no additional space to accommodate large bags. Reaching a maximum speed of 80 km/h, they can travel about 100 kilometers on a single charge. The ultra minicars also make less noise while running than conventional vehicles. The cars do not emit exhaust gases.

However, there are hurdles to clear. Industry sources say that consumers will not buy ultra minicars unless their price point is about ¥600,000 to ¥700,000, lower than that of conventional minicars.

Safety is another important issue. The small bodies of ultra minicars make it harder for drivers of larger vehicles, such as trucks, to spot them. In the event of an accident, the crash impact on an ultra minicar can be severe. Balancing safety and cost factors is expected to be one major challenge.

(*The Japan News*, August 26, 2013)

Notes
take to...「～に出る」
certify「認可する」
trial period「試用期間」
promote「推進する」
boast「誇る」
emission「排出」
equipped with...「～を装備した」
additional「余分の」
accommodate「収容する」
charge「充電」
exhaust gases「排気ガス」
industry sources「業界消息筋」
price point「小売価格」
spot「気づく」
crash impact「衝突の衝撃」
factor「要因」
challenge「課題」

* The Land, Infrastructure, Transport and Tourism Ministry（国土交通省：超小型車の公道走行は制限があるが、2013年1月の国土交通省の規制緩和によって、メーカーの超小型車開発は加速するだろう）、New Mobility Concept（NMC）（ニュー・モビリティ・コンセプト：日産の試作車の超小型EV車）

Understand what you read

本文を読んで、1と3は英文を完成し、2は本文の内容に合うように質問に答えましょう。

1. The Japanese government is keen to promote ultra minicars because
   a) they will collect more tax on fuel.
   b) they are more environmentally-friendly.
   c) they will boost the Japanese economy.
   d) they take up less road space.

2. Which of the following statements about the New Mobility Concept is NOT true?
   a) It can travel about 100 kilometers per charge.
   b) It is quieter than a traditional car.
   c) It can carry up to two passengers and their suitcases.
   d) It does not release any gases into the atmosphere.

3. In order for the ultra minicars to sell well, the makers will have to
   a) keep the ultra minicar price higher than that of conventional minicars.
   b) provide strong safety features.
   c) persuade the government to make a separate lane for bigger vehicles.
   d) reduce the numbers of larger vehicles on the roads.

Summarize what you read

本文の内容に合うように、(　　) 内に選択肢から適当な語を選んで書き入れましょう。

> The Japanese government has allowed some car (1.　　　　　) to begin road-testing ultra minicars, which are very compact electric cars that can seat up to two (2.　　　　　). Although some (3.　　　　　) regarding safety and costs remain, it is expected that the ultra minicars will help lower carbon dioxide (4.　　　　　).

manufacturers　　concerns　　emissions　　people

Get to know engineering genres

Target Genre ▶ **Table**

新製品の性能などを表にまとめると、製品の特徴を比較するのに便利です。表中には**句や複合名詞**が使用され、**簡潔な表現**が工夫されます。

以下の例と表を参照しながら1〜3の文章中の下線部に適当な語句を書き入れましょう。

E.g. An elephant is ___bigger than___ a mouse. (big)

1. The Coms is _____ the MC-β. (slow)

2. The New Mobility Concept is _____ the Coms. (fast)

3. The New Mobility Concept can travel _____ the MC-β on a single charge. (far)

Major ultra minicar models
Travel distances after full charge

Company	Toyota Auto Body Co.	Nissan Motor Co.	Honda Motor Co.
Model	Coms	New Mobility Concept	MC-β
Maximum speed	60 km/h	80 km/h	More than 70 km/h
Distance	About 50 km	About 100 km	More than 80 km
Main features	One-seat EV being sold as category-1 motorbike	Two-seat EV. Based on Renault SA model sold in Europe	EV providing cabin space that fits two adults comfortably

Chapter 5

進化するポータブル・デバイス

機械・電気

What's new?

音声を聞いて、写真の製品（地図やEメールが表示できる時計）を説明している英文をa～cから選びましょう。

Learn useful sci-tech expressions

音声を聞いて、1～5の（　　）内に適当な単語を書き入れましょう。

1. data-processing (　　　　　　　　)　　［データ処理能力］
2. image-(　　　　　　) device　　　　　［画像投影装置］
3. voice (　　　　　　)　　　　　　　　　［音声認識］
4. (　　　　　　　)　　　　　　　　　　　［設計する］
5. (　　　　　　　)　　　　　　　　　　　［無線で］

Learn engineering English tips

科学技術を紹介する新聞記事やレポートでは、技術を一般の人にわかりやすく説明するために技術を表す語句の後にダッシュ記号（—）を用いて、その技術を詳しく説明することがあります。

以下の英文で紹介されている日本企業が開発中の下線部の「ウェアラブル・テクノロジー」について、どのような技術なのか具体例を挙げながら説明しましょう。

Companies in Japan are developing "wearable technology" — used for items such as wristwatches and eyeglasses with data-processing capabilities.

Get information

Japan, overseas firms battle over wearable tech business

Companies in Japan and overseas are accelerating their development of "wearable technology" — used for items such as wristwatches and eyeglasses with data-processing capabilities.

South Korea's Samsung Electronics is expected to announce a new watch-type device soon. Google, based in the United States, has generated considerable buzz over its Google Glass product. The prototypes released by Google work via voice recognition to execute tasks such as getting directions or translating words, with the information being displayed on a tiny screen in front of the right eye.

And with domestic makers including Sony hurrying to enter this market, competition over the next generation of computing devices is expected to heat up.

Sony plans to release its SmartWatch 2 next month. The device is designed to connect wirelessly with a user's smartphone to send and receive e-mails, display maps, and function as a music player.

QD Laser, a start-up firm based in Kawasaki and capitalized in part by Fujitsu, has developed an image-projection device that sits inside the frame arm of a pair of eyeglasses.

The device emits a laser that is reflected on a part of the lens, projecting the image directly onto the wearer's retina. The technology allows even people with poor vision to see clear images or enjoy videos.

The company plans to have the device on the market by the end of fiscal 2015. "We want to sell it worldwide for less than the cost of a smartphone," QD Laser President Mitsuru Sugawara said.

(*The Japan News*, September 2, 2013)

Notes

accelerate「加速させる」

generate considerable buzz over...
「〜にかなり夢中になる」
release「発表する」
execute「行う」

domestic「国内の」

start-up「新興の」
capitalize「出資する」
frame arm「ツル」
emit「発する」
reflect「反射する」
retina「網膜」
poor vision「弱視」

fiscal「会計年度の」

＊ Samsung Electronics（サムスン電子）、QD Laser（QD レーザ社：高効率半導体レーザを用いた製品の開発メーカー、代表取締役菅原充氏）

Understand what you read

本文を読み、質問に答えましょう。

1. How does Google Glass work?
   a) A person types in information that is displayed on a tiny screen.
   b) A person speaks to the device and it does what the person says.
   c) The device translates the information from the screen.
   d) The device instructs the user via voice commands.

2. Which Sony SmartWatch 2 function is NOT mentioned in the aritcle?
   a) Makes calls   b) Plays music   c) Shows maps   d) Sends emails

3. Which of the following statements about QD Laser's image-projection device is true?
   a) The device is inside the lens of the eyeglasses.
   b) This technology is just for people with poor vision.
   c) The image is projected directly onto the eye.
   d) Images can be displayed, but not videos.

Summarize what you read

本文の内容に合うように、(　　) 内に選択肢から適当な語を選んで書き入れましょう。

> Japanese and overseas companies are (1.　　　　　) to enter the wearable technology market. For example, the US's Google is (2.　　　　　) eyeglasses that can execute voice commands and Japan's QD Laser's eyeglasses function by (3.　　　　　) images onto a person's retina. South Korea's Samsung and Japan's Sony are each (4.　　　　　) on releasing "smart" watches in the near future.

projecting   competing   working   developing

Get to know engineering genres

Target Genre ▶ **Advertisement**

企業広告は見る人を引きつけるために、レイアウトや文字に工夫を凝らしますが、企業や技術の紹介文では、**インパクトのある語彙を使用**するなどの特徴が見られます。

以下は、QD レーザ社の HP からの抜粋です。日本語訳を参考にして、(　　) 内に選択肢から適当な語句を選んで書き入れましょう。

HOME
Company
Products
Applications
Technology
Distribution partners
Support
Press release

WELCOME to QD Laser

QD Laser Inc. is a (1.　　　　　) provider of (2.　　　　　) semiconductor laser solutions for Telecom/Datacom, consumer electronics, and industrial use. We (3.　　　　　) ourselves in the market place by our product values such as finely tuned wavelengths from 532 nm to 1310 nm and high-temperature operation and stability. Our products (4.　　　　　) help our customers create new laser light markets in a variety of applications such as LAN / FTTH, optical interconnection, material processing, etc.

　　highly-efficient　　　reliably　　　leading　　　distinguish

日本語訳：量子ドットレーザ技術の先駆者としてスタートした QD レーザは、通信・民生・産業用の広い分野で高効率半導体レーザソリューションをお客様にお届けします。QD レーザの製品には、精密制御された 532nm から 1310nm までのレーザ波長、市場において高温動作と温度安定性という他社にない特長があります。信頼性の高い当社製品をお使いいただくことによって、LAN/FTTH、光インタコネクト、材料加工等の多様なアプリケーション分野で、お客様はレーザを活用した新たな市場を開拓することが可能となります。

(QD レーザ日本語 HP より、一部改変)

Chapter 6

癌を検知する「賢いメス」

医療工学

What's new?

音声を聞いて、写真（臓器をレーザで切り取ったときに生じる煙で癌ができているかどうかを検知できる新型外科ナイフを使って、豚の肝臓で実験している）を説明している英文をa～cから選びましょう。

Photo：AP

Learn useful sci-tech expressions

音声を聞いて、1～5の（　　）内に適当な単語を書き入れましょう。

1. radiation（　　　　　　）　　［放射線治療］
2. operating（　　　　　　）　　［手術台］
3. make（　　　　　）　　　　　［確認する］
4. （　　　　　　　）　　　　　［除去する］
5. （　　　　　　　）　　　　　［実験的な］

Learn engineering English tips

大きな数字を読む時は、数字を区切っているコンマの所にまとまった数字を表す語を入れながら読みます。

1～4の数字の読み方を示した語句の（　　）内に適当な語を書き入れましょう。

1. 120,000,000,000　→　one hundred and twenty（　　　　　　　　）
2. 5,000,000　　　　→　five（　　　　　　　）
3. 250,000　　　　　→　two（　　　　　　　）and fifty（　　　　　　　）
4. 380,000　　　　　→　（　　　　　）（　　　　　　　）and（　　　　　　）（　　　　　　　）

Get information

New surgical knife can detect cancer instantly

Surgeons may have a new way to smoke out cancer. An experimental surgical knife can help surgeons make sure they have removed all the cancerous tissue, doctors reported on Wednesday. Surgeons typically use knives that heat tissue as they cut, producing a sharp-smelling smoke.

The new knife analyzes the smoke and can instantly signal whether the tissue is cancerous or healthy.

Dr. Zoltan Takats of Imperial College London suspected the smoke produced during cancer surgery might contain some important cancer clues. So he designed a "smart" knife hooked up to a refrigerator-sized mass spectrometry device on wheels that analyzes the smoke from cauterizing tissue.

The smoke picked up by the smart knife is compared to a library of smoke "signatures" from cancerous and non-cancerous tissues. Information appears on a monitor: green means the tissue is healthy, red means cancerous and yellow means unidentifiable.

Currently, surgeons send samples to a laboratory to make sure they have removed the tumor while the patient remains on the operating table. It can take about 30 minutes to get an answer in the best hospitals, but even then doctors cannot be entirely sure, so they often remove more tissue than they think is strictly necessary. If some cancerous cells remain, patients may need to have more surgery or undergo chemotherapy or radiation treatment.

The new knife and its accompanying machines were made for about £250,000 ($380,000), but scientists said the price tag would likely drop if the technology is commercialized.

(by Maria Cheng, Associated Press, July 17, 2013)

* Imperial College London（インペリアル・カレッジ・ロンドン：ロンドンに本部を置くイギリスの公立大学）

Understand what you read

本文を読んで1と2は質問に答え、3は本文の内容に合うように英文を完成させましょう。

1. How is Dr. Takats' new knife different from other surgical knives?
   a) It produces smoke as it cuts through tissue.
   b) It offers quicker analysis of whether the tissue is cancerous.
   c) It reduces the smell of burning tissue to aid analysis.
   d) It is linked to a refrigerating unit which reduces the heat produced.

2. Which of the following statements about the current method of surgery is NOT true?
   a) The tests are carried out before the operation.
   b) It can take longer than half an hour to get the test results back.
   c) Surgeons are not able to know for certain whether they have removed all of the cancerous material.
   d) Some patients may need a course of chemotherapy after surgery.

3. The price of the new technology
   a) means most hospitals cannot afford it.
   b) will definitely increase in the future.
   c) is lower for scientists.
   d) could decrease if it were mass-produced.

Summarize what you read

本文の内容に合うように、(　　) 内に選択肢から適当な語を選んで書き入れましょう。

> A new type of surgical (1.　　　　　) has been developed that cancer surgeons could use to dramatically reduce the time it takes for them to test whether all cancerous (2.　　　　　) has been removed. Surgical knives use (3.　　　　　) to cut and the new technology takes advantage of this. It analyzes the smoke which is produced and compares its makeup to existing (4.　　　　　) on cancerous and non-cancerous tissue almost instantaneously.

heat　　knife　　data　　tissue

Chapter 6　医療工学　29

Get to know engineering genres

Target Genre ▶ **Note-taking**

講義を聞いてノートをとる場合、できるだけ**数字や固有名詞など忘れてしまいやすい情報は必ずメモ**します。また話の骨子は文章でメモするのではなく、**句や節単位で簡潔に**情報の流れをまとめることが重要です。

 以下は本文で紹介された外科メスに関する講義の一部を聞いた学生の講義ノートの一部です。音声を聞いてメモ中の間違いを3つ見つけましょう。

Testing the knife

・Created database of 3000＋ molecular profiles of cancerous smoke

・Tried the knife (2001-2013) @ 3 hospitals

・Compared smoke from 19 operations with database

・100% success rate

・Published in "Science Translation Medicine"

Chapter 7

緊急時に「光る」モノ

化　学

What's new?

音声を聞いて、写真の製品（蛍光色に光るゲル）を説明している英文をa〜cから選びましょう。

ⓐ　ⓑ　ⓒ

提供：朝日新聞社

Learn useful sci-tech expressions

音声を聞いて、1〜5の（　　　）内に適当な単語を書き入れましょう。

1. fluorescent (　　　　　　　) gel　　［蛍光発光ゲル］
2. oxidizing (　　　　　　)　　　　　　［酸化剤］
3. chemical (　　　　　　)　　　　　　［化学反応］
4. (　　　　　　　　)　　　　　　　　［溶液］
5. (　　　　　　　　)　　　　　　　　［光化学］

Learn engineering English tips

> 物質の特性を表す語句は技術文書にはよく出てきます。基本的なものは覚えておきましょう。

次の1〜4の物質の特性を表す語の意味を選びましょう。

1. softness　　　　　　(　　　　　　)
2. hardness　　　　　　(　　　　　　)
3. stickiness, viscosity (　　　　　　)
4. elasticity　　　　　　(　　　　　　)

　　　伸縮性　　　粘着性　　　柔らかさ　　　硬さ

31

Get information

Hakko Giken, university jointly develop luminescent gel

SAGA—Hakko Giken Co. and Saga University have developed a fluorescent light-emitting gel that could help save lives in emergencies by providing a long-lasting source of illumination that can be seen from a great distance. "This gel can be used to call for help in a disaster," said Toichi Kojima, Hakko Giken president.

The new technology is also expected to be used in art and school activities. "I'd like people to use it as an educational tool that helps children become interested in science," he said.

The company has already applied for a national patent for the new technology. Hakko Giken previously created a solution that emits light by blending an oxidizing agent and a fluorescent agent to form a chemical reaction. However, that mixture had drawbacks as it would trickle down walls and seep into the soil and dried-up grass.

Since April 2012, Hakko Giken has worked with Kenichi Nakashima, a physical chemistry professor at Saga University, Graduate School of Science & Engineering. Nakashima has been conducting research in photochemistry and the viscosity of substances. After experimenting with many combinations using various agents, they finally found a mixing method that retained its luminescent properties even in gel form.

The texture of the light-emitting gel ranges from a mayonnaise-like softness to a bean paste-like stickiness, and the light emission time can be adjusted from 0.5-16 hours.

When placing the gel into a thin plastic 0.2-square-meter bag, for example, the gel conforms to the shape of the bag and emits a square light, which can be seen up to one kilometer away in the dark.

(*The Asahi Shimbun*, Sep. 3, 2013)

Notes

luminescent「発光する」

in emergencies「緊急時に」
long-lasting「長時間持続する」
source of illumination「光源」

apply for...「〜を出願する」
patent「特許」
previously「以前」
fluorescent agent「蛍光剤」
drawback「難点」
trickle down「たれる」
seep into...「〜に染み込む」

agent「溶剤」
retain「維持する」
property「特性」
texture「感触」

adjust「調節する」

conform to...「〜と同じになる」

Understand what you read

本文を読み、質問に答えましょう。

1. What is the purpose of making the gel?
   a) To help save people's lives in an emergency
   b) To provide illumination for Saga University
   c) To get a national patent

2. What was the problem with the previous mixture?
   a) It dried up grass.
   b) It destroyed the soil.
   c) It went down walls.

3. Which one of these points is NOT true about the Hakko gel mixture?
   a) The gel mixture can take the shape of the object it is placed in.
   b) The gel can be seen more than one kilometer away at night.
   c) The gel's light can be adjusted to last for up to sixteen hours.

Summarize what you read

本文の内容に合うように、(　　) 内に適当な語を選択肢から選んで書き入れましょう。

> Hakko Giken Company and Saga University have joined together to develop a gel that produces a long-lasting light. The gel's light can be seen from a (1.　　　　) distance and (2.　　　　) to last for hours. The (3.　　　　) mixture went down walls; however, since April 2012, a new, improved texture was developed. The developers hope that this technology can be used for emergencies or in schools to help students to become (4.　　　　) in science.

adjusted　　interested　　previous　　far

＊ Hakko Giken Co.（株式会社発光技研：代表取締役、小島　十一氏）、Saga University, Graduate School of Science & Engineering（佐賀大学大学院工学系研究科）

Get to know engineering genres

Target Genre ▶ **Email**

Email は情報交換にはなくてはならないツールです。**Subject（件名）**はメールの内容の簡潔な要約となるよう工夫し、本文は **Dear Mr./Ms./Prof. 相手の姓**で始めます。最後に **Sincerely/Best Wishes** などを**結語**として用い、**自分の名前、肩書き、所属**などを記載します。

次の email を読み、内容に合うように以下の 1 ～ 4 の文章の（　　　）内の適当な語句を選びましょう。

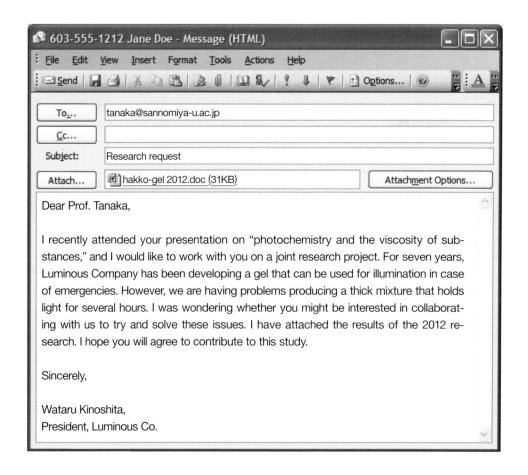

1. The main purpose of the email is to (complain about / request help with) the gel.
2. Prof. Tanaka and Mr. Kinoshita have (not worked / worked) jointly for 7 years.
3. Luminous Company has been (successful / unsuccessful) in creating a thick enough gel.
4. Prof. Tanaka probably works in the (Chemistry / Literature) Department of a university.

Chapter 8

超電導リニア登場

電気・機械

What's new?

音声を聞いて、写真（山梨県でテスト運行をする新幹線）を説明している英文をa～cから選びましょう。

ⓐ ⓑ ⓒ

提供：読売新聞社

Learn useful sci-tech expressions

音声を聞いて、1～5の（　　）内に適当な単語を書き入れましょう。

1. (　　　　　　　　)　　［磁気浮上式の］
2. (　　　　　　　　)　　［革新的特徴］
3. (　　　　　　　　)　　［標高］
4. (　　　　　　　　)　　［勾配］
5. sound (　　　　　　)　　［防音壁］

Learn engineering English tips

接続詞の as には、時や理由を表す用法のほかに、「～するにつれて～」の用法があります。どの用法なのかは、個々の文脈から判断しなくてはなりません。

次の1～3の as は、「時」「理由」「～につれて」のうちそれぞれどの用法でしょうか。（　　）内に用法を書き入れましょう。

1. (　　　　) Regular railways cannot climb more than 30 meters per kilometer since the ability of a train's wheels to "grab" the tracks decreases **as** speed increases.
2. (　　　　) **As** we arrived, we could see the students had already finished the experiment.
3. (　　　　) **As** the new train runs through tunnels, riders can't enjoy the view.

Get information

Deep secrets of maglev Shinkansen emerging

The Linear Chuo Shinkansen, a dream ultraexpress maglev train system that will likely come into use in 2027, features a variety of unique innovations.

One thing Central Japan Railway Co. (JR Tokai) is especially proud of concerning the railway tracks used for the maglev train system is its technology that overcomes a great difference of elevation of up to 1,300 meters—from a maximum of 100 meters underground in Tokyo to a tunnel 1,200 meters high near the Southern Japanese Alps.

The Linear Shinkansen's biggest selling point is its speed, which exceeds 500 kph. To make best use of this point, the railway operator selected the shortest route possible to Nagoya. Along the route, however, sit the giant mountains of the Southern Japanese Alps. The Linear Shinkansen will climb these mountains using technology that is better than any other bullet train.

Regular railways cannot climb more than 30 meters per kilometer since the ability of a train's wheels to "grab" the tracks decreases as speed increases. The Linear Shinkansen, however, is expected to mount steep inclines of 40 meters per kilometer around the border of Kanagawa and Yamanashi prefectures.

The new train will run through tunnels and under concrete sound barriers, which will largely prevent riders from enjoying the view. One solution is to place small windows at regular intervals in the sound barriers so that customers see what would look like an unbroken view of the outside scenery, somewhat like a flip-book comic. JR Tokai is considering using this idea in sections of the route where Mt. Fuji is visible.

(*The Japan News*, Oct. 14, 2013)

Notes

railway track「線路」

selling point「セールスポイント」
make best use of「〜を最大限に利用する」

mount「登る」
steep「急な」

flip-book comic「パラパラ漫画」

Understand what you read

本文の内容に合うものにはT（True）を、合わないものにはF（False）を（　　）内に書き入れましょう。

1. (　　) The highest tracks on the line are at 1,300 meters.

2. (　　) The route to Nagoya was chosen because of its giant mountains.

3. (　　) The new Linear Shinkansen can climb 40 meters per kilometer.

4. (　　) The new train will have no windows to see outside scenery.

5. (　　) JR Tokai is thinking about making it possible for riders to see Mt. Fuji.

Summarize what you read

本文の内容に合うように、（　　）内に選択肢から適当な語を選んで書き入れましょう。

> A fast new Shinkansen (**1.**　　　　　) is scheduled to debut in 2027. The first (**2.**　　　　　) being developed, from Tokyo to Nagoya, is the shortest, but also has a 1,300 meter climb. New (**3.**　　　　　) being used, however, will allow the train to climb elevations of 40 meters per kilometer, 10 meters higher than regular trains over the same distances. Although the train will mainly run through tunnels and under concrete sound barriers, JR Tokai wants to find some way to allow its customers to appreciate the (**4.**　　　　　).

scenery　　system　　route　　technology

Get to know engineering genres

> **Target Genre** ▶ **Instructions**
>
> 機械操作などの指示をする文には、基本的に**命令形**が用いられます。形式は「命令文」ですが、「〜しなさい」といった命令のニュアンスはなく、日本語の「〜してください」にあたります。

 以下の"How to buy tickets"の手順を参考にしながら、チケットの買い方を指示している会話を聞き、以下の問いに答えましょう。

How to buy tickets

Tickets can be purchased at JR Ticket Offices, JR TOKAI TOURS, and major Japanese travel agencies.

[JR Ticket Offices]　　　　　　　　　　　　[JR TOKAI TOURS]

Purchase procedure

Provide the agent with the following information:

(1) Departure station, destination (station)
(2) Date and time of boarding
(3) Type of train (Nozomi / Hikari / Kodama)
(4) Number of persons (adult, child [6 to 12 years])
(5) Preferences (non-reserved seat / reserved seat / first-class car)

---

1. Where is the customer going?
2. When does the customer want to travel?
3. How many tickets will the customer buy?
4. What kind of seats does the customer want to buy?
5. How will the customer pay for the tickets?

Chapter 9

手のひらであなたが分かる

情報・機械

What's new?

音声を聞いて、写真（手のひらの静脈の画像の一部）に写っている曲線を説明している英文をa～cから選びましょう。

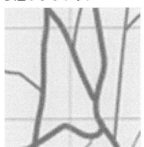

ⓐ　ⓑ　ⓒ

Learn useful sci-tech expressions

音声を聞いて、1～5の（　）内に適当な単語を書き入れましょう。

1. (　　　　　　　　)　　　　　　　　　　［数字］
2. palm (　　　　　　　) authentication　　［手のひら静脈認証］
3. (　　　　　　) data　　　　　　　　　　［生体データ］
4. (　　　　　　　　)　　　　　　　　　　［人物特定］
5. (　　　　　　) code　　　　　　　　　　［特徴コード］

Learn engineering English tips

科学技術系の文章では誤解のないように物事を正確に言い表す必要があります。読み手を考慮して、あいまいな表現を避ける工夫が必要です。特に図形の言い表し方は覚えておくといいでしょう。

以下の形を表す語の英語を選択肢より選んで（　）内に書き入れましょう。

1. 立方体（　　　　　　　）　4. 三角形（　　　　　　　）
2. 楕円形（　　　　　　　）　5. 長方形（　　　　　　　）
3. 円錐形（　　　　　　　）　6. 正方形（　　　　　　　）

　　　square　　cone　　oval　　triangle　　cube　　rectangle

Get information

A new palm vein ID system creates codes for multiple services

Fujitsu Ltd. has developed new palm vein authentication technology that creates numberless "feature codes" for authentication from biometric data of palm vein images, the company said. A conventional palm vein identification system has been widely used at banks, hospitals and other facilities for security purposes, and 40 million people worldwide have registered data.

Like fingerprint authentication technology, the palm authentication also adopts a system where a sensor reads vein patterns, which are different for each person and can be utilized as an individual code for identification. However, the current system has issues that need to be addressed. First, the images are not processed before being authenticated which makes the system less secure. In addition, due to the use of only one image at different locations or for various services, there are concerns that an image obtained through unauthorized access could be used for criminal purposes.

Fujitsu's new technology will eliminate such security concerns. Fujitsu developed a system where the vein images are divided into several tens of square shapes. Information such as the number of veins and direction of blood flow in veins is extracted for each square-shaped image and assigned codes using "0" and "1." The codes for all images are then converted into a string of 2,048-bit feature codes.

Due to the large number of digits in the feature codes, nearly infinite patterns of feature codes can be generated from one set of biometric data through the new system, company officials said. If one of these feature codes is leaked or stolen, one can simply generate a new feature code and continue using the service without worry.

Notes

numberless「無数の」

conventional「従来の」

adopt「採用する」

address「検討する」
process「加工する」
due to...「〜のために」
concerns「懸念」
obtain「入手する」
unauthorized
「許可されていない」
eliminate「なくす」

extract「うつし取る」
assign「割り当てる」
string「記号列」

infinite「無限の」

Fujitsu will make an effort to further increase accuracy and make the new technology available for commercial use in 2015.

accuracy「精度」
make...available for commercial use「〜を実用化する」

(*The Asahi Shimbun*, Sep. 13, 2013)

Understand what you read

本文の内容に合うものにはT (True) を、合わないものにはF (False) を (　　) 内に書き入れましょう。

1. (　　) There are security concerns with the conventional palm vein ID system.

2. (　　) Forty million people have used the conventional palm vein ID system.

3. (　　) If someone steals a feature code in the new system, a new one can be generated.

4. (　　) The new technology is available for commercial use before 2015.

Summarize what you read

本文の内容に合うように、(　　) 内に選択肢から適当な語を選んで書き入れましょう。

> Fujitsu Ltd. has created new palm identification technology that (1.　　　　　) more secure and accurate than the current ID system. The new system, available from 2015, (2.　　　　　) a person's palm vein patterns and blood flow and converts the information into feature codes. This (3.　　　　　) a person to securely access multiple services using different feature codes. If someone (4.　　　　　) the feature codes, new ones can be easily generated.

reads　　allows　　is　　steals

Get to know engineering genres

Target Genre ▶ Process chart

プロセスを表す図版において、英文の説明の中にはしばしば**動詞で始まる文**が使われますが、命令文ではないので気をつけましょう。

以下は手のひらの静脈を使った認証システムの仕組みを説明した図です。図を参考にしながら音声を聞いて、以下の文章の空所1〜3に適当な語を書き入れましょう。

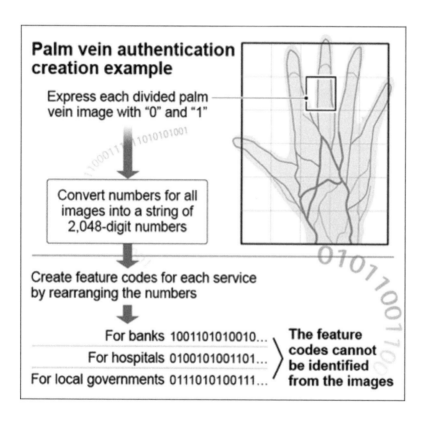

How are images of palm veins turned into feature codes? First, each divided palm vein image is (1.   ) with "0"s and "1"s. Next the numbers for all the images are (2.   ) into strings of numbers that are 2,048 digits long. For each service, for example, a bank or a hospital, separate feature codes are (3.   ) by rearranging the numbers.

Chapter 10

国際基準を作って産業育成

医療工学

What's new?

音声を聴いて、介護ロボットの国際基準について説明しているものをa～cから選びましょう。

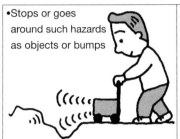

- Stops or goes around such hazards as objects or bumps

- Does not retain heat or produce static electricity after long periods of use

  ⓒ

Learn useful sci-tech expressions

音声を聞いて、1～5の（　　）内に適当な単語を書き入れましょう。

1. (　　　　　　　) production　［大量生産］
2. (　　　　　　　) standard　［安全基準］
3. static (　　　　　　　)　［静電気］
4. (　　　　　　　)　［まとめる］
5. (　　　　　　　)　［機能］

Learn engineering English tips

「名詞 + V-ed（過去分詞）/ V-ing（現在分詞）」のような、形容詞相当語句で名詞を後ろから修飾する構文は技術文書では多用されます。

1～3の名詞を修飾するのに適したものをa～cから選びましょう。

1. criteria (　　　)　　2. patients (　　　)　　3. robots (　　　)

   a) suggested by Japan
   b) designed to assist the elderly
   c) using nursing care robots

Get information

ISO to adopt Japan-led safety criteria for nursing-care robots

The International Organization for Standardization (ISO) will compile global safety standards in September for nursing-care robots based on criteria proposed by Japan, paving the way for domestic mass production and exports. The latest move is widely expected to foster a new industry based on robot technology, which the government explained as part of its growth strategy to rebuild the country's economy.

The establishment of ISO standards will also give a boost to the full-fledged production and export of devices manufactured by Japanese companies. The ISO, founded in 1947, is a private organization that sets international standards for industrial products. It currently has 163 member states.

The safety criteria suggested by Japan will be adopted by the ISO and used as the basis for more than 80 sections to outline safety standards for robots designed to assist the elderly and those in need of special care. Subsequently, private certification bodies of the ISO member states will conduct tests on products in accordance with each section.

Nursing-care robots are designed to fulfill various functions to help patients live independently and therefore reduce the burden on caretakers. ISO sections will likely require that nursing-care robots can detect uneven floors, objects, humans and animals, so that collisions are avoided, while ensuring that equipment does not tip when used by patients.

The ISO safety standards will also require the installation of a device, among other systems, to reduce noise and vibration, and to release static electricity and heat safely.

(*The Japan News*, July 29, 2013)

Notes

criteria「基準」
pave the way for…
「〜の道を開く」
foster「育てる」

give a boost to…
「〜を後おしする」
full-fledged「本格的な」

adopt「採用する」
outline
「要点をまとめる」
subsequently「その後」
certification body
「認証団体」
in accordance with…
「〜に従って」
fulfill「実行する」

caretaker「介護者」
uneven「段差のある」
collision「衝突」
ensure「保証する」
tip「倒れる」

among other…
「〜の中でも特に」
release「発散する」

* International Organization for Standardization（国際標準化機構 ISO：産業の分野で国際的な標準化を推進している組織）

Understand what you read

本文を読んで、1と3は質問に答え、2は本文の内容に合うように英文を完成させましょう。

1. Which of the following statements is true?
   a) Japan is drawing up guidelines based on the ISO's recommendations.
   b) Domestic production of nursing-care robots has declined.
   c) Japan founded the ISO in 1947.
   d) The new standards will boost Japanese exports.

2. After the standards are finalized, the private certification bodies in ISO member states will
   a) use them to assess products.
   b) give additional feedback to the ISO.
   c) be reduced to 80.
   d) be able to start designing nursing-care robots.

3. Which of the following possible requirements for the nursing-care robots is NOT mentioned in the article?
   a) able to sense other objects around them
   b) able to pick themselves up if they fall over
   c) able to emit any heat that builds up
   d) able to minimize vibrations

Summarize what you read

本文の内容に合うように、（　　）内に選択肢から適当な語を選んで書き入れましょう。

Japan has given a number of suggestions regarding the specifications of nursing-care robots to the ISO, which will (1.　　　　) them to create new global safety standards. The safety standards will (2.　　　　) requirements for such robots to be able to (3.　　　　) obstacles and people, remain stable and minimize noise. It is hoped that the emerging industry will (4.　　　　) to support Japan's economic recovery.

include　　help　　avoid　　use

Chapter 10　医療工学

Get to know engineering genres

Target Genre ▶ **News broadcast**
新聞やテレビやインターネットなど、さまざまなメディアでニュースは報道されます。ニュース放送の場合、最初の部分で**ニュースの背景の概略**が紹介されますので、最初の部分の聞き取りが肝心です。

 Get information のセクションは、英字新聞のニュース記事ですが、同じニュースを取り上げたラジオ放送の冒頭の部分を聞いて以下の質問に答えましょう。

1. According to the news announcer, what percentage of Japan's population will be 65 or over by 2055?
   a) Just under 14%
   b) Just over 14%
   c) Just under 40%
   d) Just over 40%

2. What are listeners likely to hear next?
   a) The next news story
   b) An interview
   c) A story about Catherine Thornton
   d) The opinion of the head of the ISO

Chapter 11

もはや「運転手」はいらない？

電子

What's new?

音声を聴いて、写真（自動運転装置を搭載した試作車に男性が乗っている）を説明している英文を a～c から選びましょう。

ⓐ　ⓑ　ⓒ

Learn useful sci-tech expressions

音声を聞いて、1～5の（　　）内に適当な単語を書き入れましょう。

1. (　　　　　　) car　　［試作車］
2. (　　　　　　)　　　　［行う］
3. (　　　　　　)　　　　［自動制御］
4. (　　　　　　)　　　　［自動運転装置］
5. (　　　　　　)　　　　［実現可能性］

Learn engineering English tips

技術文書では、複数の語をハイフンで結んだ複合形容詞の使用が数多く見られます。

日本語を参考に、1～3の（　　）内に入る語を選択肢から選んで書き入れましょう。

1. (　　　　)-driving　　　［自動運転の］
2. (　　　　)-board　　　　［車内搭載の］
3. not-(　　　　)-distant　［あまり遠くない］

too　　self　　on

Get information

Nissan rolls out self-driving car at Japanese electronics show

CHIBA—Nissan Motor Co. conducted a demonstration of its futuristic self-driving car on Oct. 1 at the Ceatec Japan 2013 consumer electronics show.

In the first public demonstration of its capabilities in Japan, the prototype car, running at speeds of a little less than 20 kph, stopped at stop signs, used the correct turning and lane changing signals, handled curves and navigated around other cars, all with a driver who never touched the wheel.

The secret behind its automation are sensors and five on-board cameras. The sensors detect other vehicles, traffic signals and road signs, enabling the car to navigate roads and traffic.

The automaker plans to market a self-driving vehicle by 2020 in countries around the world. It plans to start testing the car on public roads in the not-too-distant future.

Self-driving cars are expected to someday help prevent accidents, ease traffic congestion and assist those who have difficulty driving, such as the elderly.

Nissan said it intends to further improve the car's ability to detect obstacles and navigate roads before it goes commercial. Though the price has yet to be decided, a senior Nissan official said the automaker will make every effort to keep the new car affordable.

Currently, drivers are banned under Japanese law from operating vehicles on autopilot on public roads. The transport ministry has set up a commission that consists of auto industry officials and experts to look into the feasibility and under what conditions such vehicles will be allowed to travel on public roads.

(*The Asahi Shimbun*, Oct. 2, 2013)

Notes
roll out「初公開する」
capability「将来性」
turning and lane changing signal「方向指示・車線変更灯」
wheel「ハンドル」
public road「公道」
ease「緩和する」
congestion「渋滞」
obstacle「障害物」
go commercial「市販する」
affordable「入手しやすい」
currently「現在」
ban「禁止する」
commission「委員会」

＊ Ceatec Japan（シーテックジャパン：毎年10月に開催されるアジア最大級の最先端IT・エレクトロニクス国際展示会」、the transport ministry（国土交通省）

Understand what you read

空所に入る適当な語を本文から選び、質問に対する答えを完成させましょう。

1. Q: Where was the Ceatec Japan held?
   A: It was held in (   ).

2. Q: How does this Nissan self-driving car work?
   A: It uses (   ) and on-board (   ).

3. Q: When will Nissan start to test the car on public roads?
   A: It will start in the near (   ).

4. Q: Is it possible to use self-driving cars in Japan at present?
   A: No, it is against the (   ).

Summarize what you read

本文の内容に合うように、(   ) 内に選択肢から適当な語句を選んで書き入れましょう。

Nissan has created a prototype of a self-driving car that uses sensors and cameras to drive the car, (1.   ) the need for a human driver. Self-driving cars, (2.   ) could be marketed by 2020, are seen to have many benefits (3.   ) increased safety. The autopilot cars, (4.   ), are not yet legal on Japan's streets. The government is looking into what is needed to change the law.

   which   such as   however   without

Get to know engineering genres

> **Target Genre** ▶ **Registration**
> 展示会や研究発表会などに出席する場合、事前登録を求められる場合があります。登録に関連する**頻出単語**（pre-registration, admission fee, on-site など）**の理解**が必要となります。

以下の CEATEC JAPAN 2013 の事前登録案内を読み、内容に合うものには T（True）を、合わないものには F（False）を（　　）内に書き入れましょう。

Pre-registration

Pre-registration online eliminates the need to register on-site at the event and enables free admission.

Pre-registration online enables free admission (admission fees at the event site: JPY 1,000 general, JPY 500 students) and it also means that there is no need to register on-site at the event, making things much more convenient when you arrive.

* Print out the email with Admission Pass prior to coming to the show. Please note that the Admission Pass will not be mailed by postal service.

1. (　　) 'Pre-registration' means registering before the event takes place.
2. (　　) You will get free admission if you register on-site at the event.
3. (　　) Pre-registering online means students only pay 500 yen.
4. (　　) If you pre-register, you need to print and bring the admission pass to the show.

Chapter 12

親離れする日は近い？!

機械

What's new?

音声を聞いて、写真（魚の形をしたロボット）を説明している英文をa～cから選びましょう。

ⓐ　ⓑ　ⓒ

Learn useful sci-tech expressions

音声を聞いて、1～5の（　　　）内に適当な単語を書き入れましょう。

1. (　　　　　　　　)　　　　　［知覚］
2. (　　　　　　　　)　　　　　［操縦する］
3. (　　　　　　　　) sensor　　［赤外線センサー］
4. (　　　　　　　　)　　　　　［器用さ］
5. (　　　　　　　　)　　　　　［監視］

Learn engineering English tips

名詞を表わす接尾辞はいろいろありますが、例えば -th は寸法を表す名詞によく使われるので、覚えておくと仕様書などを書く際に役立ちます。

次の形容詞を名詞に変化させましょう。

1. deep　→（　　　　　　）「奥行き」
2. wide　→（　　　　　　）「幅」
3. strong→（　　　　　　）「強度」
4. long　→（　　　　　　）「長さ」

Get information

Robots are getting closer to having humanlike abilities and senses

WASHINGTON — It may seem uncomfortably close to science fiction, but robots are moving ever nearer to acquiring humanlike abilities to see, smell and sense their surroundings, allowing them to operate more independently and perform some of the dangerous, dirty and dull jobs people do not want to do.

They can smell gas leaks, conduct underwater surveillance and even sort boxes by shape and color and toss them into the appropriate warehouse bin. Advances in sensor technology and software allow these machines to make split-second decisions without human masters overseeing actions such as how to follow a scent trail or where to go to next.

Until now, robots have had to navigate via small infrared sensors that keep them from bumping into things. Some have relied on video cameras that send images to human operators. However, a new generation of robots is gaining the ability to understand voices, see objects with the same depth of perception as humans and use grasping arms with dexterity closer to that of humans.

Most robots with advanced sensing abilities are still in the experimental stage. More than toys but not yet tools, they work well in the laboratory but cannot yet handle real-world situations.

Stanford University computer science professor Gary Bradski, co-founder of Industrial Perception, a start-up that invents labor-saving robots for tasks involving sensitive decisions, said "It's getting the speed and reliability to make it economic. You can't fail very often; otherwise, you're not saving any labor."

(by Eric Niiler, *The Washington Post*, Aug. 5, 2013)

Understand what you read

本文を読み、1の英文を完成させ、2と3の質問に答えましょう。

1. According to the article, some robots can
   a) create a dangerous situation.
   b) operate in water.
   c) crush old packaging.
   d) allow operators to make quick decisions.

2. According to the article, how is the new generation of robots different to the previous ones?
   a) They can send images more quickly to the operators.
   b) They no longer bump into objects.
   c) They can sense things in a more human-like way.
   d) They can be fitted with more arms.

3. What does the Stanford University professor say about robots?
   a) Robots are better than humans in speed and reliability.
   b) Robots are great inventions that help economic growth.
   c) Robots that are consistently reliable will save on labor.
   d) Robots that have advanced sensing abilities are toys.

Summarize what you read

本文の内容に合うように、(　　　)内に選択肢から適当な語を選んで書き入れましょう。

Recent advances in (1.　　　　　　) have allowed robots to become more humanlike in how they make sense of their (2.　　　　　　) and in their movements. Although these new robots have shown significant (3.　　　　　　), they are still not ready for life in the (4.　　　　　　) world. Stanford University professor Gary Bradski explains that robots need to be more reliable if they are to replace human workers.

environment　　real　　progress　　technology

Get to know engineering genres

Target Genre ▶ Demonstration

商品のデモンストレーションやプレゼンテーションは、論文とは違い、目の前にいる聴衆に対して行われます。**分かりやすい言葉**で、聴衆の反応を見ながら、**特徴の紹介**がなされます。

次の写真を見ながら、ガスボットというロボットのデモンストレーションの音声を聞き、以下の1～5の文章が内容と合っていればT（True）、間違っていればF（False）を（　　）内に書き入れましょう。

1. (　　) Gasbot is a lawn mower with an eyeball.
2. (　　) Gasbot can travel on various kinds of surfaces.
3. (　　) Gasbot's purpose is to find and identify smells.
4. (　　) Gasbot uses three laser beams to pick up smells.
5. (　　) Gasbot helps to protect humans from gas leaks.

Chapter 13

気体の錬金術で夢の新材料を

化 学

What's new?

音声を聞いて、写真（ある物質のモデルを使って化合物が生成される様子）を説明している英文をa〜cから選びましょう。

ⓐ　ⓑ　ⓒ

Learn useful sci-tech expressions

音声を聞いて、1〜5の（　）内に適当な単語を書き入れましょう。

1. (　　　　　　　)　［真空］
2. (　　　　　　　)　［分子］
3. (　　　　　　　)　［原子］
4. (　　　　　　　)　［分解する］
5. (　　　　　　　)　［合成する］

Learn engineering English tips

'hold' という動詞は、理工系分野において重要な多義語のひとつです。主要な意味として、1)「物をしっかりとつかむ」、2)「〜の容量がある」、3)「会議などを開催する」、4)「考え・ルールなどがあてはまる」などがあります。

1〜4の文における hold の意味は上の 1)〜4)のどれにあたるでしょうか。（　）内に数字を書き入れましょう。

1. This bottle holds two liters of water.　(　　)
2. Please hold the handrail and mind your step.　(　　)
3. Moore's law still more or less holds true.　(　　)
4. The next international conference will be held from August 12 to August 14.　(　　)

Get information

Nanotech scientist aspires to master 'alchemy of gases'

OSAKA—A 62 year-old Kyoto University professor, Susumu Kitagawa, won the 10th Leo Esaki Award for his outstanding research in nanotechnology. He created a chemical compound called "porous metal complex," which has many cavities, each measuring one nanometer, or one-billionth of a meter, across.

"We may be able to create resources by putting different molecules and atoms into these holes to decouple or synthesize them," Kitagawa said, as he demonstrated by putting a ball into a model of the substance he created.

When Kitagawa saw a substance he accidentally created during an experiment, he thought "I can use this for something." It is common knowledge in the science world that porous substances from organic molecules are very unstable. However, after many experiments, he developed a method that allowed the substance to maintain its shape even in a vacuum.

His article on porous coordination polymers has been cited over 20,000 times by researchers around the world.

Kitagawa also successfully carried out an experiment in which targeted molecules can be put into the cavities of a porous coordination polymer to change the size and shape of the cavities. If research progresses, it may become possible to extract carbon, hydrogen and oxygen from the atmosphere, and synthesize fuel. "I want to master the 'alchemy of gases,' and with this new mastery I would then be in control of gases," he said.

"Usefulness of uselessness," a phrase said to be from the Chinese philosopher Zhuangzi, is one of Kitagawa's favorites. It means that something seen as useless may actually be important. "The idea holds true in science as well," Kitagawa said. "The cavities of my chemical compound are exactly that."

(*The Japan News*, Sep. 25, 2013)

Notes

aspire「熱望する」
alchemy「錬金術」
outstanding「卓越した」
chemical compound「化合物」
porous metal complex「多孔性配位高分子」
cavity「細孔」

porous substance「多孔性物質」
organic molecule「有機分子」
unstable「不安定な」
maintain「維持する」
porous coordination polymer「多孔性配位高分子」
cite「引用する」
carry out「行う」

extract「取り出す」

mastery「技、技能」
be in control of...「〜を制御する」

exactly that「まさにそれ」

Understand what you read

本文の内容に合うものにはT (True) を、合わないものにはF (False) を（　　）内に書き入れましょう。

1. (　　) The compound that Mr. Kitagawa created has a large number of holes.
2. (　　) Mr. Kitagawa created the substance on purpose during his experiment.
3. (　　) The research that Mr. Kitagawa has done has been read by many other scientists.
4. (　　) Mr. Kitagawa has successfully synthesized fuel.
5. (　　) Mr. Kitagawa said that his chemical compound's cavities are really useless.

Summarize what you read

本文の内容に合うように、（　　）内に選択肢から適当な語を選んで書き入れましょう。

> An award winning Kyoto University professor has created a new porous chemical (1.　　　　　) with many small cavities. Porous substances are known to be unstable. However, the professor developed a new (2.　　　　　) that allowed the porous substance to keep its (3.　　　　　), even in a vacuum. The professor's future (4.　　　　　) might involve synthesizing fuel and extracting hydrogen and oxygen from the atmosphere.

method　　research　　shape　　compound

＊ Leo Esaki Award（江崎玲於奈賞：ナノテクノロジー分野において顕著な研究業績を挙げた者に与えられる賞）、Zhuangzi（荘子：中国戦国時代の思想家）

Get to know engineering genres

Target Genre ▶ **Presentation slides of lectures**

講義で提示されるプレゼンテーションのスライドは、講義内容を分かりやすくするために、短いフレーズでまとめられています。とりわけ**新しい用語の定義**は重要です。用語の定義を表す構文、A is B や A means B といった構文に注意しましょう。

次のスライドは、$2H_2 + O_2 \rightarrow 2H_2O$ のような化学反応式 (chemical equations) に関する講義の一部をまとめたものです。音声を聞き、(　　) 内に入る語を書き入れましょう。

Reactants:
　　written on the (1.　　　　　) side of the arrow

Products:
　　written on the (2.　　　　　) side of the arrow

⟶ :
　　means to (3.　　　　　) or make

Chapter 14

再生可能エネルギー導入拡大への鍵

電気・エネルギー

What's new?

音声を聞いて、写真（世界最大の蓄電池システム）を説明している英文をa～cから選びましょう。

ⓐ　ⓑ　ⓒ

Learn useful sci-tech expressions

音声を聞いて、1～5の（　）内に適当な単語を書き入れましょう。

1. (　　　　　　　) battery　［蓄電池］
2. power (　　　　　　　)　［発電］
3. (　　　　　　　)　［変電所］
4. (　　　　　　　)　［生産能力］
5. life (　　　　　　　)　［寿命］

Learn engineering English tips

新しい技術が開発されると、それまで不可能だったことが可能になります。そんなときは、既存の動詞に「～ができる」という意味の -able という接尾辞を付けて新しい意味を表すことがよくあります。次のような語が典型的な例です。

　　renew（再生する）　+ able → renewable（再生可能な）
　　wear　（身につける）+ able → wearable　（ウエアラブル）

次の1～4に該当する語を選択肢から選びましょう。

1. 使い捨ての　　　　　（　　　　　　　）
2. 再充電可能な　　　　（　　　　　　　）
3. 調節可能な　　　　　（　　　　　　　）
4. 消すことのできる　　（　　　　　　　）

　　　disposable　　　erasable　　　adjustable　　　rechargeable

Get information

Big battery eyed as green energy cure

Japan will build the world's largest storage battery system in Hokkaido as early as autumn of 2013 in a bid to rectify fluctuations in the electricity produced by renewable energy sources. The project is aimed at promoting renewable energy by addressing a key defect—inconsistent power generation.

The electricity generated by such sources accounts for only 1.6 percent of the nation's total, partly because solar and wind power are affected by the changes in the weather.

To raise renewable energy's role in the national energy mix, the Ministry of Economy, Trade and Industry pushed for the development of a large storage system that would store electricity when weather conditions are favorable and dispense it when the weather fails.

Sumitomo Electric Industries Ltd. and Hokkaido Electric Power Co. are leading the storage project, and the ministry has provided ¥20 billion to cover all development and manufacturing costs.

For the project, Hokkaido Electric will build what is called a "redox flow" battery system, produced by Sumitomo, at a substation in the town of Abira. With a capacity of 60,000 kwh, the system will be as high as a six-story building.

A redox flow battery repeats charging and discharging operations in a tank, using an electrolytic solution of vanadium. While it is safe and has a life span of 10 to 20 years, it can be readily converted into a large system, experts say.

The ministry believes that using such batteries will allow utilities to buy 10 percent more electricity from green energy sources.

(*The Japan Times*, Sep. 25, 2013)

* the Ministry of Economy, Trade and Industry（経済産業省）、energy mix（エネルギー・ミックス：特定の発電方法に偏らず、それぞれの特性を活かしてバランス良く組み合わせ、安定して電気を作ること）

Understand what you read

本文の内容に合うものにはT (True) を、合わないものにはF (False) を（　　）内に書き入れましょう。

1. (　　) According to the article, renewable energy is a consistent source of electricity.
2. (　　) Renewable energy is only a small part of Japan's electricity generation.
3. (　　) The Japanese government is helping to pay for the storage system.
4. (　　) The storage battery system will be housed in six buildings.
5. (　　) Sales of renewable energy will probably increase if the batteries are used.

Summarize what you read

本文の内容に合うように、（　　）内に選択肢から適当な語を選んで書き入れましょう。

　　Japan is to build the (1.　　　　　　) largest storage battery system in an effort to address a key concern of renewable energy and inconsistent power generation. With the (2.　　　　　　) backing, (3.　　　　　　) battery storage system will store energy in good weather and release energy in times of need. The "redox flow" battery has a vanadium solution, a life span of up to 20 years, and the (4.　　　　　　) capacity is 60,000 kwh.

Hokkaido's　　government's　　world's　　system's

Get to know engineering genres

Target Genre ▶ **Note-taking**

講義を受講する時、その内容をすべて書き写すことはできませんので、重要な情報を見直したときに分かりやすいようにメモしておかなければなりません。ひとつの方法として、**「質問」と「答え」の形式**に情報をまとめておくと効果的です。

次はある学生のノートです。音声を聞いて（　　　）内に適切なものを選択肢から選びましょう。

Japan's energy supply　　　　About (1.　　　) % from oil
The transportation sector　　Almost (2.　　　) % from oil

Why?
Because there are so many (3.　　　) cars.

The government's new goal
The transportation sector　　(4.　　　) % from oil by (5.　　　)

100　　80　　50　　2030　　gasoline-powered　　electric

Chapter 15

新しい生命体を作り出す企業

バイオ

What's new?

音声を聞いて、写真（バイオテクノロジー企業の最高経営責任者ジャック・ニューマン氏）を説明している英文を a ～ c から選びましょう。

ⓐ　ⓑ　ⓒ

Learn useful sci-tech expressions

音声を聞いて、1 ～ 5 の （　　） 内に適当な単語を書き入れましょう。

1. life-form / （　　　　　　　　）　　　　　［生命体］
2. （　　　　　　　　）　　　　　　　　　　　［実験室］
3. （　　　　　　　　）　　　　　　　　　　　［細胞］
4. （　　　　　　　　）（　　　　　　　　）　［DNA 配列］
5. （　　　　　　　　）　　　　　　　　　　　［石油化学製品］

Learn engineering English tips

「～につき」という意味を表す表現には '1,000 yen an hour'（1 時間に 1,000 円）のように前置詞を省略する用法もありますが、'per week' や 'by the day' のように前置詞を使うものもあります。

次の 1 ～ 4 の（　　）内に当てはまるものを選択肢から選びましょう。必要なければ×を書き入れましょう。

1. The maintenance engineer works 8 hours (　　) a day.
2. The rental fee of the device costs 2,000 yen (　　) week.
3. The researcher gets paid (　　) the hour.
4. This science magazine is published twice (　　) a month.

per　　by

63

Get information

Scientists now creating millions of organisms from scratch

WASHINGTON—For scientist Jack Newman, creating a new life-form has become as simple as this: He types out a DNA sequence on his laptop, and clicks "send." Nearby in the laboratory, robotic arms start to mix together some compounds to produce the desired cells.

Newman's biotech company is creating new organisms, mostly forms of genetically modified yeast, at a dizzying rate of more than 1,500 a day. Some convert sugar into medicines. Others create moisturizers that can be used in cosmetics. And still others make biofuel, a renewable energy source usually made from corn.

"You can now build a cell the same way you might build an app for your iPhone," said Newman, chief science officer of Amyris.

Some believe this kind of work marks the beginning of a third industrial revolution — one based on using living systems as "bio-factories" for creating substances that are too tricky or too expensive to grow in nature or to make with petrochemicals.

The rush to biological means of production promises to revolutionize the chemical industry and transform the economy, but at the same time it also raises questions about environmental safety and bio-security and revives ethical debates about "playing God." Hundreds of products are in the pipeline.

Since it was founded a decade ago, Amyris has become a legend in the field that sits at the intersection of biology and engineering, creating more than 3 million new organisms. Unlike traditional genetic engineering, which typically involves swapping a few genes, the scientists are building entire genomes from scratch.

(*The Washington Post*, Oct 27, 2013)

* Amyris（アミリス社：米国のバイオ化学品企業）

Notes

from scratch「ゼロから」

robotic arm「ロボットアーム」
desired「意図した」
biotech「バイオテクノロジーの」
genetically modified yeast「遺伝子組み換え酵母」
dizzying「目の回るような」
convert「改造する」
moisturizer「保湿剤」
biofuel「バイオ燃料」

tricky「手の込んだ」

revolutionize「大変革をもたらす」
raise「提起する」
revive「再燃させる」
play God「神のようにふるまう」
be in the pipeline「生産中である」
intersection「交差点」
genetic engineering「遺伝子工学」
involve「関わる」
entire genome「ゲノム全体」

Understand what you read

本文の内容に合うものには T (True) を、合わないものには F (False) を (　) 内に書き入れましょう。

1. (　) The main purpose of this article is to inform you of a biotechnology company that is creating new organisms.
2. (　) Now you can build a cell or a new organism with an iPhone application.
3. (　) According to the article, there are no ethical issues with this new technology.
4. (　) Amyris creates more than 1,500 identical organisms a day.
5. (　) Using this technology, hundreds of products are now being made.

Summarize what you read

本文の内容に合うように、(　) 内に選択肢から適当な語を選んで書き入れましょう。

A biotech company has (1.　　　　) over 3 million new organisms using computers and robots. The company has (2.　　　　) a symbol of a new kind of genetic engineering by building entire genomes from scratch. There has (3.　　　　) criticism concerning the ethics of creating new life forms. On the other hand, hope has (4.　　　　) for a new revolution in the chemical industry.

been　　　arisen　　　become　　　created

Get to know engineering genres

Target Genre ▶ **Corporate profile**

企業のHP上の企業概要（HP上では以下のように"About＋企業名"といった形式で示されるケースが一般的）では、事業活動、決算資料のほか、環境へのとりくみ、商品・サービスなどについてまとめられています。こうした性質上、企業概念には **「AはBである」といった定義文** が比較的多く用いられる傾向があります。

ABOUT AMYRIS

Amyris is a renewable products company providing sustainable alternatives to a broad range of petroleum-sourced products. Amyris applies its industrial synthetic biology platform to convert plant sugars into a variety of molecules — flexible building blocks that can be used in a wide range of products.

Notes: sustainable「持続可能な」

 ケンとエリコが就職活動について話しています。上の企業情報を参照しながら会話を聴き以下の問いに答えましょう。

1. What kind of company is Amyris?
   a) A company that creates new plant sugars
   b) A company that makes new molecules
   c) A company that makes advertisements for cosmetics
   d) A company that builds new laboratories

2. Who found a job?
   a) Eriko   b) Ken   c) Both Eriko and Ken   d) Neither person

3. What kind of job did the person get?
   a) Mechanical engineer
   b) Plant engineer
   c) Systems engineer
   d) Chemical engineer

Chapter 16

スパコンで天気予報

電子

What's new?

音声を聞いて、写真（地球の表面の雲の動き）を説明している英文をa～cから選びましょう。

2012年8月25日 NICAM（水平解像度0.87km）

ⓐ　ⓑ　ⓒ

提供：理化学研究所

Learn useful sci-tech expressions

音声を聞いて、1～5の（　　）内に適当な単語を書き入れましょう。

1. (　　　　　　　　)　　　［正確な］
2. essential (　　　　　　)　　　［不可欠な要素］
3. weather (　　　　　　)　　　［天気予報］
4. atmospheric (　　　　　　)　　　［大気の状況］
5. (　　　　　　　　)　　　［気象学の］

Learn engineering English tips

理工系の英語では、名詞や形容詞とまったく同じ形の動詞が少なくありません。意味的にも、その名詞や形容詞と密接に関連しています。

次の1～3の（　　）内に適切な語を選択肢から選び、必要であれば適切な形に直しましょう。

1. High-tech supercomputers could (　　　　　　) each block down to 3.5 kilometers.
   ハイテクのスーパーコンピュータは各ブロックを3.5キロメートル四方にまで狭めることができた。

2. The problems started to (　　　　　　) in the 1980s.
   1980年代に問題が表面化し始めた。

3. Researchers have (　　　　　　) the genome of a spider for the first time.
   科学者たちは、クモのゲノムを初めて解読した。

　　　　map　　narrow　　surface

Get information

Japanese supercomputer shows detailed cloud movements on Earth's surface

A group of scientists have created a detailed cloud map of the Earth's surface using the K computer — Japan's fastest processing supercomputer — that could help provide more accurate forecasts for typhoons and heavy rain.

With a cloud map, the Earth's surface is divided into square blocks. Cloud formation and movement, which are essential factors in weather forecasts, are predicted based on atmospheric conditions in each block. Typically, computers at meteorological institutions such as the Japan Meteorological Agency divide each block into squares measuring 20 km × 20 km. Previous attempts to use high-tech supercomputers have been able to narrow each block down to 3.5 kilometers.

However, by using the K computer, a team of scientists from RIKEN, the Japan Agency for Marine-Earth Science and Technology (JAMSTEC) and the University of Tokyo, were able to split the Earth's surface into some 63 billion hexagonal blocks, with each block spaced only 870 meters apart, and successfully reproduced cloud movement in each block.

When the team tested the system to reproduce cloud movement during Typhoon No.15 in August 2012, which devastated the Amami Islands in Kagoshima Prefecture, the cloud map showed a detailed picture of clouds across the entire globe. RIKEN scientist Hirofumi Tomita said the team will work on improving the system for more accurate typhoon and heavy rain forecasting as there has been an increase in such natural disasters.

Notes
surface「表面」

square「正方形の」
formation「形成」
predict「予測する」

split「分ける」
hexagonal「六角形の」
reproduce「再現する」

devastate「多大な被害を与える」
entire「全体の」
work on…「〜に取り組む」
natural disaster「自然災害」

(*The Mainichi*, Sep. 23, 2013 ［一部改変］)

＊ the Japan Meteorological Agency（気象庁）、RIKEN（独立行政法人理化学研究所）、the Japan Agency for Marine-Earth Science and Technology（独立行政法人海洋研究開発機構）【補足】気象庁は中心から中心までの距離が 20 km の 4 角形に分割した画像データを使うが、理研のチームでは中心から中心までの距離が 870 m の 6 角形に分割される。

Understand what you read

本文の内容に合うものにはT (True) を、合わないものにはF (False) を (　　) 内に書き入れましょう。

1. (　　) Scientists are using a supercomputer to help predict the weather.
2. (　　) Cloud formations are important to consider when making weather forecasts.
3. (　　) There were about 63 billion cloud movements over the Earth's surface.
4. (　　) The K computer uses weather information from small areas to guess cloud formations.
5. (　　) The system was tested and will be further improved.

Summarize what you read

本文の内容に合うように、(　　) 内に選択肢から適当な語を選んで書き入れましょう。選択肢は文頭にくる語も小文字で示しています。

(1.　　　　　　) Japan's fastest supercomputer, scientists have created a cloud map of the whole world. Predicting cloud formation and movement is done by (2.　　　　　　) areas of land into blocks. Then the computer uses weather information from each block to forecast cloud formations. Scientists tried (3.　　　　　　) cloud movements from a typhoon in 2012. They are (4.　　　　　　) on making the forecast system better and more accurate.

working　　　reproducing　　　using　　　dividing

Get to know engineering genres

> **Target Genre** ▶ **Homepage**
> ホームページの情報は**タイトルや見出しごとにわかりやすく分類され、名詞で表される**のが一般的です。自分が探したい情報を効率よく見つけるためにも、**名詞表現**に慣れておきましょう。

以下は気象関連のホームページの情報です。1〜5の状況の場合、どのタブをクリックしたらよいか、〔　　〕内に番号を書き入れましょう。

Weather homepage

- National weather
  - ○ Today's forecast　①
  - ○ 3-day forecast　②
  - ○ Weekly forecast　③
- Regional weather
  - ○ Today's forecast　④
  - ○ 3-day forecast　⑤
  - ○ Weekly forecast　⑥
- Atmospheric pressure　⑦
- Wind speed　⑧
- Air pollution　⑨
- UV index　⑩

- Weather warnings
  - ○ Flooding　⑪
  - ○ Typhoons　⑫
  - ○ Landslides　⑬
  - ○ Snow　⑭
  - ○ Tsunami　⑮
  - ○ Volcanic eruptions / ash　⑯

---

1. Today is Tuesday and you want to know about the weather for the whole of Japan on the weekend.〔　　〕
2. You want to know how much sun protection you will need today.〔　　〕
3. You want to know more about a blizzard that your friends told you about.〔　　〕
4. Today is Friday and you want to know about the weather in your area tomorrow.〔　　〕
5. You want to know about today's air quality.〔　　〕

Chapter 17

スマホと嗅覚の香しい関係

機 械

What's new?

音声を聞いて、写真（香拡散器が装着されているスマートフォン）を説明している英文をa～cから選びましょう。

ⓐ　ⓑ　ⓒ

Learn useful sci-tech expressions

音声を聞いて、1～5の（　　　）内に適当な単語を書き入れましょう。

1. （　　　　　　　）　　　［操作する］
2. high-（　　　　　　）　　［高解像度の］
3. （　　　　　　　）　　　［付属品］
4. （　　　　　　　）　　　［拡散する］
5. （　　　　　　　）　　　［カートリッジ］

Learn engineering English tips

接尾辞の -er, -or は動詞を名詞化し、「～する人、～するもの、～する機械」という意味になります。動詞とセットで覚えておくと語彙力が倍増します。

次の1～3の語に -er または -or の接尾辞をつけて、名詞に変化させましょう。

1. diffuse → （　　　　　）
2. adapt → （　　　　　）
3. sense → （　　　　　）

Get information

Firm wants your smartphone to be able to smell

　　When operating a smartphone, three of the five senses are used: touch (manipulating the screen), hearing (listening to music or a show — or just participating in that old-fashioned activity known as a phone call) and sight (viewing photos or video on the high-resolution display).

　　The other two senses — taste and smell — may not come into play, but Tokyo-based Scentee Inc. wants to change that. It is releasing a gadget to the market next month that will make smell a part of the smartphone experience.

　　The attachment, also called the Scentee, emits a scent in accordance with how the phone is being used. It is believed to be the world's first such device for smartphones.

　　The device, which is plugged into the earphone jack, has a tank that can puff out a scent about 100 times. The Scentee can act as a simple scent diffuser if the user sets the device to spray automatically at specific times, for instance when one is getting up in the morning.

　　Currently, the firm is planning two business models with the Scentee, said Koki Tsubouchi, Scentee Chief Executive Officer. One is to sell cartridges of various aromas, such as rose, lavender, jasmine and strawberry. They will be priced at ¥500, and the company plans to let third parties produce them as well by selling them empty cartridges. The Scentee itself will be sold at ¥3,480.

　　The other is to collect data on when and where people diffuse what kind of scent and then build a big database from the collected data. Once this database is created, they expect many companies doing business related to scents to come calling.

(*The Japan Times*, Oct 16, 2013)

Notes

five senses「五感」

come into play「関わる、関与する」

release「発売する、出す」
gadget「機器」

emit「発する」
in accordance with...「〜に従って」

be plugged into...「〜に接続される」
puff out「出す」

Chief Executive Officer
= CEO「最高経営責任者」

third party「サードパーティ」

＊ Scentee Inc.（着パフ株式会社：東京を拠点とするIT関連企業）

72

Understand what you read

本文を読み、1と2の質問に答え、3の英文を完成させましょう。

1. How is the Scentee expected to operate on a smartphone?
   a) A diffuser which emits scents will be connected to the smartphone adapter.
   b) Two smartphones will be connected to the Scentee attachment.
   c) A tank will be connected to the smartphone's earphone jack.
   d) Several scent cartridges will be connected to the attachment.

2. How does Scentee Inc. hope to use third parties in their business plan?
   a) Scentee Inc. will sell them cartridges filled with various scents.
   b) Third parties will collect data of popular scents for Scentee Inc.
   c) Third parties will be responsible for manufacturing cartridges for Scentee Inc.
   d) Scentee Inc. will sell third parties unfilled cartridges.

3. The expression "come calling" in the last sentence of the passage could be replaced with
   a) "copy them."
   b) "diffuse them."
   c) "approach them."
   d) "sue them."

Summarize what you read

本文の内容に合うように、(　　) 内に選択肢から適当な語を選んで書き入れましょう。

Scentee Inc. plans to (1.　　　　　) a scent gadget that will make smell a part of the smartphone experience. The company presently has two business models. The first model is to sell cartridges with various scents. Third parties will (2.　　　　　) provided with empty cartridges to (3.　　　　　) with their own scents. The second is to create a database of when and where scents are used. They hope that these business models will (4.　　　　　) companies.

release　　　attract　　　be　　　fill

Chapter 17　機械　73

Get to know engineering genres

Target Genre ▶ **Meeting**

　ミーティングにおいては、"What (how) about...?" や "Let's talk about..." など、**議論に必要な特有の表現**を心得ているとスムーズにディスカッションできます。

「香りを放つ携帯電話」の利用法についてアイデアを出し合っている短い会議の内容を聞いて、質問に答えましょう。

1. Where is this meeting probably taking place?
    a) At a company that wants to produce cartridges for the Scentee
    b) At the company that produces the Scentee
    c) At one of Scentee's main rivals
    d) At a trade fair for perfume manufacturers

2. Which statement best describes the woman's opinion?
    a) She thinks the company should go forward with the man's idea.
    b) She thinks they need scents that appeal to younger consumers.
    c) She thinks it will be impossible to manufacture the cartridges.
    d) She thinks the idea does not appeal enough to men.

3. What will the man do next?
    a) Try to develop a sweeter scent to appeal to teenage girls
    b) Test a herb-based cartridge for the Scentee
    c) Get more information about the cost of the cartridges
    d) Gather data about what groups of people might own Scentee devices

Chapter 18

高齢化社会に強力な助っ人

機械

What's new?

音声を聴いて、イラストを説明している英文をa〜cから選びましょう。

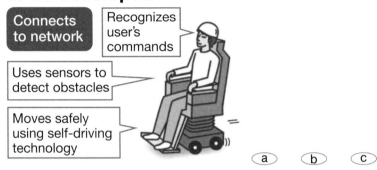

Learn useful sci-tech expressions

音声を聞いて、1〜5の（　）内に適当な単語を書き入れましょう。

1. (　　　　　　　　　　　)　　　　　　　　　［活用する］
2. (　　　　　　　　) technology　　　　　　　［先端技術］
3. (　　　　　　　　) system　　　　　　　　　［神経系］
4. (　　　　　　　　　　　)　　　　　　　　　［情報通信］
5. home (　　　　　　　) (　　　　　　　)　　［家庭用電化製品］

Learn engineering English tips

テクノロジーやシステムなどの説明には、「テクノロジー / システム ＋（前置詞）＋関係代名詞」がよく使われます。

以下の1と2の英文の（　）内に共通する前置詞を書き入れましょう。

1. Technologies needed for robot wheelchairs include a system (　　　　　) which computers recognize users' intentions when the users think about a direction.
2. Telecommunication technology, (　　　　　) which multiple wheelchairs will be connected by networks, enables users to share information.

Get information

Robot wheelchairs would read users' minds

The Internal Affairs and Communications Ministry said it aims to start a project to develop "robot wheelchairs," which detect the users' intentions from their brain waves and automatically move in line with the users' will.

5 　While the graying of Japan's population continues, the ministry expects that robot wheelchairs will be put to practical use in nursing care facilities, where a labor shortage is predicted.

　In cooperation with research institutes, telecommunications companies and machinery manufacturers, the ministry aims to put 10 the technology to practical use possibly in 2017. The planned robot wheelchairs will have sensors that detect users' intentions by analyzing their brain waves and nervous system activity, moving automatically.

　Some research institutions, such as Advanced Telecommunications 15 Research Institute International based in Kyoto Prefecture, have studied technologies needed for the robot wheelchairs. They include a system in which computers recognize users' intentions if users think about the directions, for example right or left, in which they want to move. In their experiments, wheelchairs have 20 successfully moved short distances and performed simple operations involving home electronic appliances.

　The ministry also plans to establish telecommunication technology in which multiple wheelchairs will be connected by networks so that their users will be able to share information 25 about obstacles and uneven surfaces. Under the planned system, wheelchairs will calculate current locations and routes to destinations. The latest information from wheelchairs that have passed through dangerous places will be sent to other wheelchairs to help them choose routes that avoid danger.

(*The Japan News*［抜粋］, Aug 31, 2014)

Notes

intention「意図」
in line with...
「～に沿って」
graying「高齢化」

nursing care facility
「老人ホーム」
predict「予想する」

multiple「多数の」

uneven「段差のある」

latest「最新の」

Understand what you read

本文を読み、1～3の英文を完成させましょう。

1. The robot wheelchairs detect the users' commands by reading
   a) their voices.
   b) their brain waves.
   c) their hands.
   d) their helpers.

2. During the trial, the wheelchairs succeeded in
   a) traveling a long distance.
   b) connecting with each other using networks.
   c) operating home electronic appliances.
   d) receiving the latest information from users.

3. According to the article, the wheelchairs will be able to
   a) move things that are in the user's way.
   b) physically link together.
   c) calculate the cheapest route to a location.
   d) share data concerning uneven paths.

Summarize what you read

本文の内容に合うように、(　　) 内に選択肢から適当な語を選んで書き入れましょう。

> The Internal Affairs and Communications Ministry plans to (1.　　　　　) developing "robot wheelchairs" which might be put into practical use in 2017. The wheelchairs (2.　　　　　) their users' commands and move automatically. Another ministry plan aims to (3.　　　　　) multiple wheelchairs using networks in order to enable their users to (4.　　　　　) information about dangerous places.

share　　connect　　start　　recognize

＊ the Internal Affairs and Communications Ministry（総務省）、Advanced Telecommunications Research Institute International（国際電気通信基礎技術研究所：知能ロボットなどの情報通信技術関連の先駆的研究を行っている）

Get to know engineering genres

Target Genre ▶ Interview

英語でインタビューされたときは、**Wh questions** か **Yes-No questions** かを聞き分け、答えのスタイルを決めます。

音声を聴いて、ThinkChair という架空のロボット車椅子に関する以下のインタビューの下線部に入る適当な語を書き入れましょう。

Interviewer : Thanks for trialing the new ThinkChair and agreeing to talk to us. You've been a wheelchair user for about three years. Is that right?

Interviewee : 1)_____ ! That's right.

Interviewer : And 2)_____ long did you test the ThinkChair for?

Interviewee : About two weeks.

Interviewer : As a wheelchair user, 3)_____ did you think about the ThinkChair?

Interviewee : It was quite good, but I had a few problems while using it.

Interviewer : 4)_____ did you experience these problems?

Interviewee : Mostly at the beginning. It took me a while to get used to just thinking and the chair moving automatically. It was strange at first and I think I needed more training.

Interviewer : OK... So maybe we need to create a better training session. But you said it was quite good. 5)_____ ?

Interviewee : Well, because the chair could tell me the shortest route to my destination and it helped me to avoid stairs along the way. That was really impressive!

Chapter 19

食品偽装を見破るソフト

情 報

What's new?

音声を聞いて、写真を説明している英文を a ～ c から選びましょう。

　ⓐ　ⓑ　ⓒ

Learn useful sci-tech expressions

音声を聞いて、1 ～ 5 の（　　）内に適当な単語を書き入れましょう。

1. (　　　　　　　)　　　　　　　　　　　　［特定する］
2. (　　　　　　　)　　　　　　　　　　　　［見破る］
3. (　　　　　　　) (　　　　　　　)　　　　［生物］
4. (　　　　　　　)　　　　　　　　　　　　［環境の］
5. (　　　　　　　)　　　　　　　　　　　　［ウイルス］

Learn engineering English tips

名詞の複数形には語尾が -s でないものも少なくありません。また、語尾が -s であっても、複数形を表しているのではない場合もあります。

次の 1 ～ 4 の語の生物の分類に関連した単語の複数形を単数形にしましょう。

1. families ［科］　　　　　(　　　　　　　　)
2. species ［種］　　　　　 (　　　　　　　　)
3. fungi ［菌類、キノコ類］　(　　　　　　　　)
4. genera ［属］　　　　　　(　　　　　　　　)

Get information

Kyoto researchers develop DNA software that can halt food fraud

 A group of researchers at Kyoto University has developed DNA barcoding software that can prevent the fraudulent mislabeling of farm products and seafood.

 Utilizing the newly developed software, users can easily determine the species of living objects based on their DNA sequence information. The development of the software was announced in the U.S. scientific research journal PLOS ONE.

 "Prices of yellowfin tuna and Pacific bluefin tuna are drastically different. But if they are used in cooking, it is difficult even for experts to distinguish between them. If you use this software, you can easily detect mislabeling," said Akifumi Tanabe, who played the central role in the software's development.

 The researchers, including those of the university's Graduate School of Global Environmental Studies, created software that can compare the DNA sequences of plants, fish and other living objects with those stored in DNA databases. By comparing the DNA barcoding, the software can automatically determine the species the tissue came from.

 Even in the case of new species, the software can determine which families or genera they belong to and which existing species they are related to.

 Databases have been released in Japan, the United States and Europe that store the DNA sequences of a total of about 288,000 species of living organisms, including fungi and viruses.

 To date, the work to determine which species living organisms belong to has mostly depended on the knowledge of experts and their experience.

(*The Asahi Shimbun*, Oct. 22, 2013)

* Graduate School of Global Environmental Studies（大学院地球環境学堂）、DNA barcoding（DNA バーコーディング手法：特定の遺伝子領域の短い塩基配列情報（DNA バーコード）を用いて生物種の同定を行う）

Notes

halt「阻止する」
food fraud「食品偽装」

fraudulent mislabeling 「悪質な不当表示」
farm products「農産物」
utilize「利用する」

DNA sequence information「DNA 配列情報」

yellowfin tuna 「キハダマグロ」
Pacific bluefin tuna 「太平洋クロマグロ」
drastically「大幅に」
distinguish「見分ける」

existing「既存の」

to date「現在までのところ」

Understand what you read

本文の内容に合うものにはT (True) を、合わないものにはF (False) を（　　）内に書き入れましょう。

1. (　　) The main purpose of this article is to warn customers about food fraud.
2. (　　) The software works by comparing the DNA sequences from a database with those from the real food.
3. (　　) Mislabeled food is easier to find with the new software.
4. (　　) New species' families can also be detected with this software.
5. (　　) Until now, only experts from Japan, the U.S. and Europe have been able to identify the species of unknown organisms.

Summarize what you read

本文の内容に合うように、（　　）内に選択肢から適当な語を選んで書き入れましょう。

Researchers from Kyoto University have developed software that can detect (1.　　　　　) labeled foods, such as seafood, that will help stop food fraud. The software works by comparing the DNA sequences of actual foods to sequences (2.　　　　　) stored in databases around the world. The software (3.　　　　　) detects the species of the product. Up until now, the process of detecting mislabeled food has (4.　　　　　) depended on the experience and knowledge of experts.

automatically　　already　　incorrectly　　commonly

Get to know engineering genres

Target Genre ▶ **Abstract**

論文のアブストラクトとは、論文の要旨を200字程度にまとめた抄録のことを言います。学術雑誌では必ず論文本体の前に掲載され、読者はまずアブストラクトでその論文を判断します。ですから研究の成果や重要性をコンパクトにまとめてアピールすることが重要です。理工系の典型的なアブストラクトの構成は、次のようになります。

①研究の背景・目的　→　②実験の方法　→　③実験結果　→　④結論

次の1～5は、異なる論文アブストラクトからの抜粋です。上で述べたアブストラクトの構成①～④のどの部分にふさわしい文章でしょうか。（　　　）内に番号を書き入れましょう。

1. The survey was completed in 2012 and all interviews were conducted over the telephone. (　　　)
2. The purpose of this study is to examine the effects of indoor heating on pets. (　　　)
3. Flammability limits of several combustible gases were measured at temperatures from 5 to 100 °C. (　　　)
4. We conclude that excessive gaming can negatively impact a number of different cognitive functions. (　　　)
5. These results indicate that our method is more efficient than the conventional method. (　　　)

Notes: flammability limit「可燃限界（可燃性のガスが燃焼するときの濃度の上限と下限）」 combustible gas「可燃性のガス」 cognitive function「認知機能」

Chapter 20

もしかして万能波長？

機械・物理

What's new?

音声を聴いて、写真（分析器によって、錠剤の表面のコーティングの厚さが均一でないという分析結果が示されている）を説明している英文をa～cから選びましょう。

ⓐ　　ⓑ　　ⓒ

Learn useful sci-tech expressions

音声を聞いて、1～5の（　　）内に適当な単語を書き入れましょう。

1. terahertz （　　　　　　　　　　） ［テラヘルツ波］
2. （　　　　　　　　　　） production ［薬剤生産］
3. （　　　　　　　　　　） ［電磁気の］
4. （　　　　　　　　　　） ［物質］
5. （　　　　　　　　　　） ［構成要素］

Learn engineering English tips

光や電気や音は、物性を分析するのに多用されます。分析結果はしばしば「波形」を使って表わされます。

次の1～6の光や電気や音の「波」に関連する語句に当てはまる日本語を選択肢から選びましょう。

1. （　　） frequency band
2. （　　） radio wave
3. （　　） penetration
4. （　　） radiation
5. （　　） generator
6. （　　） infrared ray

a) 電波　　b) 発生器　　c) 周波数帯域　　d) 放射　　e) 貫通　　f) 赤外線

Get information

Industries studying possible next big thing: Terahertz waves

Japanese companies are working on new technologies that can improve food safety, ease pharmaceutical production and thwart terrorists and drug smugglers. But one hurdle stands in the way: the unknown effects on human health.

The technologies involve the use of terahertz waves, electromagnetic radiation in the frequency band from 0.1 to 10 terahertz, which lies in the transition zone between radio waves and light.

Terahertz waves can penetrate substances as X-rays do and identify their components and types in the same manner as infrared rays. However, terahertz waves can spot things that X-rays cannot, such as paper and plastic objects, and are more penetrative than infrared rays.

These waves are found in nature, but they have long remained underused because generating them required expensive equipment or chemical agents. Advances in terahertz wave research over the past decade or so were made after a U.S. company developed an inexpensive terahertz-wave generator that uses a high-performance laser.

One possible application of the research concerns the pharmaceutical industry. Pills are often coated so that they release their components after reaching the stomach or the bowels. But uneven coating is vulnerable to cracks. The terahertz-wave analyzer shows the uneven thicknesses of the pill's surface coating.

Terahertz waves are believed to be safer than X-rays, but it is not yet known if they are toxic to human health. "Time is needed before practical applications can begin in earnest," said Iwao Hosako of Japan's National Institute of Information and Communications Technology (NICT) Terahertz Technology Research Center.

(*The Asahi Shimbun*, Oct. 26, 2013)

Understand what you read

本文の内容に合うものには T (True) を、合わないものには F (False) を (　　) 内に書き入れましょう。

1. (　　) Technologies that use terahertz waves are known to be safe for use on humans.
2. (　　) Generating terahertz waves has become less expensive in the last ten years.
3. (　　) According to the article, terahertz waves are better than X-rays at detecting paper.
4. (　　) One way the terahertz wave technology can be used is to smooth the surface of pills.
5. (　　) Terahertz technology is not yet ready for public use.

Summarize what you read

本文の内容に合うように、(　　) 内に選択肢から適当な語を選んで書き入れましょう。

　　Despite unknown health (1.　　　　　), terahertz wave technologies are advancing. There are many possible (2.　　　　　) for this research, from detecting (3.　　　　　) to improving food safety. This is because terahertz waves are better at detecting things like paper and plastic than (4.　　　　　). They are thought to be safer than X-rays as well. But more time is needed before they can be used.

　　　　X-rays　　　applications　　　effects　　　drugs

＊ National Institute of Information and Communications Technology (NICT) Terahertz Technology Research Center (独立行政法人情報通信研究機構テラヘルツ研究センター)

Get to know engineering genres

Target Genre ▶ **Diagram**

ここでは、図版中によく用いられる**桁数の大きな数字を表す接頭辞**、特に 10 の乗数を表す接頭辞を取り上げます。kilo-、mega-、giga-、tera-、peta-、exa- はそれぞれ 10 の 3、6、9、12、15、18 乗を表します。

 以下の図を参照しながら講義を聞いて、空所に適当な語句を書き入れましょう。

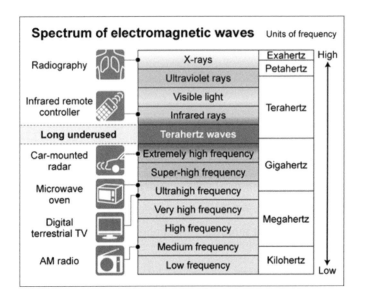

1. The electromagnetic spectrum shows the range of possible _____ of electromagnetic radiation.
2. Radio waves are measured in megahertz or _____.
3. The spectrum uses metric prefixes as the _____ of frequency, or hertz.
4. One terahertz means one _____ cycles per second.

Notes：spectrum「スペクトル：波長による分布」 metric prefix「メートル法の接頭辞」

Chapter 21

洋上風力発電は未来を照らす？

エネルギー

What's new?

音声を聴いて、写真（福島第一原子力発電所沖の海上に浮かべられている風力発電用の風車）を説明している英文をa～cから選びましょう。

ⓐ　　ⓑ　　ⓒ

Learn useful sci-tech expressions

音声を聞いて、1～5の（　　）内に適当な単語を書き入れましょう。

1. wind (　　　　　　　)　　　［集合型風力発電所］
2. (　　　　　　　) power plant　［火力発電所］
3. (　　　　　　　)　　　［再生可能（エネルギー）］
4. (　　　　　　　) power plant　［原子力発電所］
5. (　　　　　　　)　　　［電圧］

Learn engineering English tips

位置を表す表現は技術文書に多く現われます。その際、数値と組み合わされた形容詞（句）や前置詞（句）が名詞（句）を後ろから修飾するという表現が頻出します。

次の1～3の（　　）内に入る語を選択肢から選んで書き入れましょう。

1. a turbine 20 kilometers (　　　　　　　) the coast
   ［海岸から20キロメートル沖合にあるタービン］
2. seabed depths (　　　　　　　) than 50 meters　［50メートルより深い海底の深さ］
3. a seabed 120 meters (　　　　　　　)　　　［深さ120メートルの海底］

greater　　off　　deep

Get information

Japan starts up offshore wind farm near Fukushima

IWAKI, Fukushima Prefecture—Japan switched on the first turbine at a wind farm 20 kilometers off the coast of Fukushima on Nov. 11.

The wind farm near the Fukushima No.1 Nuclear Power Plant is to eventually have a generation capacity of 1 gigawatt from 143 turbines, though its significance is not limited to the energy it will produce.

Symbolically, the turbines will help restore the role of energy supplier to a region decimated by the multiple meltdowns that followed the March 2011 earthquake and tsunami. It also highlights Japan's aspirations to utilize its advanced energy technology from cleaner versions of conventional coal, oil and gas-burning thermal power plants to renewables and also nuclear power.

"We are moving ahead one step at a time. This wind farm is a symbol of our future," said Yuhei Sato, the governor of Fukushima Prefecture.

Japan, whose coast is mostly ringed by deep waters, is pioneering floating wind turbine construction, required for seabed depths greater than 50 meters. The 2 megawatt floating wind turbine that began operation on Monday is tethered to a seabed 120 meters deep. The turbine is linked to a 66 kilovolt floating power substation, the world's first according to the project operators, and an extra-high voltage undersea cable.

The project is meant to demonstrate the feasibility of locating these towering turbines in offshore regions where the winds are more reliable and there are fewer "not in my backyard" concerns—bigger turbines that might create noise problems onshore are not an issue so far offshore.

(by Elaine Kurtenbach, Associated Press, Nov. 11, 2013)

Notes
offshore「沖合の」

generation capacity「発電容量」

symbolically「象徴的に」
restore「回復する」
energy supplier「電力会社」
decimate「破壊する」
meltdown「炉心溶融」
aspiration「意気込み」

ring「囲む」
floating「浮体式の」

project operator「事業主」

not in my backyard「自己中心主義」

Understand what you read

(　　) 内に入る適当な語を選択肢から選び、質問に対する答えを完成させましょう。

1. Q: Where is the wind turbine mentioned in this article?
   A: It is floating (　　　　　　).

2. Q: What is the significance of the wind farm mentioned in this article?
   A: Besides the amount of electricity generated there, the farm is a symbol that can help restore Fukushima's role of (　　　　　　) energy to the region.

3. Q: How does the energy created in the offshore turbine reach the shore?
   A: Via an extra-high voltage (　　　　　　) under the sea.

4. Q: What is one advantage of building the wind turbines offshore?
   A: The winds are more reliable offshore than (　　　　　　).

offshore　　onshore　　cable　　supplying

Summarize what you read

本文の内容に合うように、(　　) 内に選択肢から適当な語句を選んで書き入れましょう。

> Several years after the March 2011 earthquake and tsunami, Japan has started generating power from a wind farm (1.　　　　　) km off the Fukushima coast. The site is expected to generate (2.　　　　　) gigawatt from (3.　　　　　) turbines. The turbines are connected to the world's first (4.　　　　　) kilovolt floating power substation. Offshore turbines have some advantages over onshore turbines because they generate less noise and the winds are more consistent.

66　　143　　1　　20

＊Fukushima No. 1 Nuclear Power Plant（福島第一原子力発電所）

Get to know engineering genres

Target Genre ▶ **Geographical Information**

空間や位置関係を説明する際、**方角を表す表現**が使われることがあります。そのような表現が出てきたときには、頭の中に地図をイメージしながら情報を整理しましょう。

会話を聞いて、下記の質問の答えとして適当なものを選びましょう。

1. Where does Susan currently live?
   a) Fukushima
   b) Iwaki
   c) Kansai
   d) Singapore

2. Which part of Fukushima is Iwaki City in?
   a) Northeast
   b) Southeast
   c) East
   d) West

3. How large is Iwaki City in relation to Singapore?
   a) It is larger than Singapore.
   b) It is smaller than Singapore
   c) It is the same in size as Singapore.
   d) We are not told.

Chapter 22

コンピュータが常識を持つ？

情報

What's new?

音声を聴いて、イラスト（コンピュータに常識を持たせる研究をしている研究者が、コンピュータのサーバーの前に立っている）を説明している英文を a ～ c から選びましょう。

Learn useful sci-tech expressions

音声を聞いて、1～5の（　　）内に適当な単語を書き入れましょう。

1. (　　　　　　　　) intelligence　［人工知能］
2. (　　　　　　　　)　　　　　　　［閲覧する］
3. (　　　　　　　　)　　　　　　　［再現する］
4. intelligent (　　　　　　　　)　［知的生命］
5. (　　　　　　　　)　　　　　　　［特定する］

Learn engineering English tips

科学論文においては、物体や数の大きさを表すときはできるだけ数値を明示し正確な情報を伝えなければなりません。一方、科学雑誌の記事は一般大衆向けなので、しばしば漠然と大きさを表す表現が使われます。

枠内の単語を「大きい・巨大な」という意味を持つ形容詞と、「小さい・微小な」という意味を持つ形容詞に分けましょう。

tiny　　massive　　vast　　micro　　fine　　huge

「大」（　　　　　　　　　　　　　　　　　　　　　　　　　　　　　　　　　　　　）
「小」（　　　　　　　　　　　　　　　　　　　　　　　　　　　　　　　　　　　　）

Get information

New research aims to teach computers common sense

PITTSBURGH(AP)—Researchers are trying to plant a digital seed for artificial intelligence by programming a massive computer system to browse millions of pictures and decide for itself what they all mean.

The system at Carnegie Mellon University is called "Never Ending Image Learning" (NEIL). In mid-July, it began continuously searching the Internet for images 24 hours a day and in tiny steps, started deciding for itself how the images related to each other. The research goal is to recreate what we call common sense—the ability to learn things without being specifically taught.

It is a new approach in the quest to solve computing's Holy Grail: getting a machine to think on its own using a form of common sense. The project is being funded by Google and the Department of Defense's Office of Naval Research.

"Any intelligent being needs to have common sense to make decisions," said Abhinav Gupta, a professor in the Carnegie Mellon Robotics Institute.

NEIL uses advances in computer vision to analyze and identify the shapes and colors in pictures, but it is also slowly discovering connections between objects on its own. For example, the computers have figured out that zebras tend to be found in savannahs and that tigers look somewhat like zebras. In just over four months, the network of 200 processors has identified 1,500 objects and 1,200 scenes and has connected the dots to make 2,500 associations.

Gupta is pleased with the initial progress. In the future, NEIL will analyze vast numbers of YouTube videos to look for connections between objects.

(by Kevin Begos, Associated Press, Nov. 24, 2013)

Notes

seed「種」
for oneself「自ら」

in tiny steps「少しずつ」

specifically「具体的に」
in the quest to...
「〜を追究する」
Holy Grail「至高の目標」
on its own「自力で」
fund「資金を出す」

figure out...
「〜を見つけ出す」
savannah
「サバンナ：熱帯の草原」
zebra「シマウマ」
make association
「関連づける」
initial「当初の」

Understand what you read

本文を読み、質問に答えましょう。

1. What is NEIL's purpose?
   a) To learn how to plant seeds
   b) To find millions of pictures on the Internet
   c) To identify connections among pictures on its own
   d) To analyze pictures of wild animals

2. Who is paying for the research?
   a) Carnegie Mellon University
   b) Google and the Office of Naval Research
   c) Professor Abhinav Gupta
   d) YouTube

3. Which of the following is NOT true about NEIL?
   a) It has made 2,500 connections between objects and scenes in four months.
   b) It has made connections between vast numbers of objects in a YouTube video.
   c) It has made connections between zebras and their specific surroundings.
   d) It has made connections on its own without being specifically trained for it.

Summarize what you read

本文の内容に合うように、（　　）内に選択肢から適当な語を選んで書き入れましょう。文頭にくる語も小文字で示しています。

> A computer system called Never Ending Image Learning (NEIL) searches the Internet for (1.　　　　　) 24 hours a day in order to discover (2.　　　　　) on its own. NEIL, a network of 200 computers, uses advances in computer vision to identify shapes and (3.　　　　　) in pictures and then decide for itself how they are related. (4.　　　　　) hope that this new approach will solve the problem of getting a machine to think independently.

　　　　researchers　　　colors　　　images　　　connections

*　Carnegie Mellon University（カーネギーメロン大学：ピッツバーグに本部を置く、アメリカ合衆国の私立大学）、the Department of Defense's Office of Naval Research（アメリカ国防総省内海軍研究事務所）

Get to know engineering genres

Target Genre ▶ **Comments**

科学技術関係のonline記事では、サイトによっては、コメント欄を設けてニュースの反響も発信しています。コメント欄は、**インフォーマルなライティングスタイル**のものが多くみられます。

以下は、Get information のセクションで紹介された研究に関する記事に寄せられた架空のコメントです。以下の質問の答えとして適当なものを選びましょう。

 Dave624 : Actually, IMO the human brain is just a really, really powerful computer. With enough power, it's totally possible for a computer to have "common sense." Maybe even emotions.

 Aki349 : This report is interesting but this kind of research can be very dangerous! A computer could never really develop common sense. Only human beings are capable of that kind of thinking!

 Dave624 : Hmm, I still think a computer might be able to show "common sense," though.

 Aki349 : I guess we'll have to wait and see.

Note : IMO = in my opinion

1. Aki349 thinks that
   a) it is too difficult to define "common sense."
   b) computers will always be incapable of having common sense.
   c) reading these kinds of articles can be hazardous.
   d) human brains and computers are very similar.

2. Which of the following statements is true?
   a) Aki349 was able to change Dave624's opinion.
   b) Aki349 was not able to change Dave624's opinion.
   c) Aki349 changed Dave624's opinion about the human brain.
   d) Aki349 and Dave624 were able to agree.

memo

著　者

村尾純子（むらお じゅんこ）
深山晶子（みやま あきこ）
椋平　淳（むくひら あつし）
辻本智子（つじもと ともこ）
Ashley Moore（アシュレー ムーア）
Erik Fritz（エリック フリッツ）
Tanya McCarthy（ターニャ マッカーシー）

エンジニアのための総合英語

2015 年 2 月 20 日　第 1 版発行
2023 年 8 月 20 日　第 12 版発行

編著者──村尾純子／深山晶子／椋平 淳／辻本智子
　　　　　Ashley Moore ／ Erik Fritz ／ Tanya McCarthy
発行者──前田俊秀
発行所──株式会社 三修社
　　　　〒 150-0001　東京都渋谷区神宮前 2-2-22
　　　　TEL 03-3405-4511　FAX 03-3405-4522
　　　　振替 00190-9-72758
　　　　https://www.sanshusha.co.jp
　　　　編集担当　三井るり子
印刷所──萩原印刷株式会社

Ⓒ 2015 Printed in Japan　ISBN978-4-384-33445-6 C1082
表紙デザイン──やぶはな あきお
本文イラスト・図版──田中祐介
準拠 CD 録音──ELEC
準拠 CD 制作──高速録音株式会社

JCOPY〈出版者著作権管理機構 委託出版物〉
本書の無断複製は著作権法上での例外を除き禁じられています。複製される場合は、そのつど事前に、出版者著作権管理機構（電話 03-5244-5088　FAX 03-5244-5089　e-mail: info@jcopy.or.jp）の許諾を得てください。

教科書準拠 CD 発売
本書の準拠 CD をご希望の方は弊社までお問い合わせください。